LIFE AFTER LIFE AND MEDICAL MYSTERIES

Exploring Near-Death Experiences and Life Beyond Death

Dr Francesco Chirico

© Copyright (2024) Francesco Chirico, M.D.

All Rights Deeserved

Life After Life and Medical Mysteries: Exploring Near-Death Experiences and Life Beyond Death

© Copyright (2024) All Rights Reserved

ISBN: 9798863967745

Written by Dr Francesco Chirico

Copyright Notice

No part of this book may be reproduced in any form or by any electronic or mechanical means, including information storage and retrieval systems, without written permission from the author. Recording this publication is strictly prohibited, and archiving this document is not permitted without written permission from the publisher. All rights reserved. The respective authors retain all copyrights not held by the publisher. The images in this book belong to their respective owners and are licensed to the Author on a Royalty-Free basis. All registered trademarks, service marks, product names, and features mentioned in this book are considered the property of their respective owners and are used for reference only. The use of any of these terms does not imply any endorsement

Disclaimer

The book "Life After Life and Medical Mysteries: Exploring Near Death Experiences and Life Beyond Death" is provided "as is" without any warranty, express or implied, nor any assurance of any kind. The author and the publisher make no representations or warranties regarding the accuracy, reliability, or completeness of the content, stories, or information presented. Readers should be aware that:

The stories and experiences documented in this book are based on individual perspectives and should not be considered conclusive evidence or universally applicable truths.

Although the author has taken all reasonable steps to verify the authenticity and accuracy of the stories presented, there is no guarantee that all details are complete, accurate, or representative of broader experiences.

To the fullest extent permitted by applicable law, neither the author nor the publisher will be held liable for any misunderstandings, misinterpretations, psychological distress, or other adverse effects arising from the content presented in this book.

This book is intended solely for informational and contemplative purposes and should not be used as a definitive guide about near-death experiences or life after death.

Always consult a legal professional to ensure that the disclaimer meets your needs and complies with local regulations.

Contents

Exploring Near-Death Experiences and Life Beyond Death 2

Copyright Notice 3

Disclaimer 4

Introduction 9

   My Perspective on NDEs 10

   The Scientific Method for Studying NDEs 12

   Scientific Experiments Supporting Near-Death Experiences 16

   Current Scientific Evidence 16

   The Challenges of Scientifically Approaching the Study of Near-Death Experiences 20

   The Purpose of This Book 22

Chapter 1: Between Life and Death: What Does Science Say? 25

   How widespread are these experiences? Prevalence of the Phenomenon and Differences Between NDEs and "NDE-like" Experiences 26

   Definition and Causes of NDEs 27

   Medical Conditions Associated with NDEs 28

   NDEs and Self-Defining Memories (SDM) 29

   From Psychology to Spirituality 31

   What Happens After an NDE? 33

   Impact of NDEs on Doctors, Patients, Families, and Caregivers 34

   End-of-Life Contact with Deceased Loved Ones 36

   From Naturalism to a Holistic Dimension of Medicine 37

   Scientific Interpretations of Near-Death Experiences (NDEs) .. 39

A Critical Reflection on Near-Death Experiences: Between Neurobiology and Psychological Theories 40

The Materialist and Spiritual Views of NDEs 41

How Are NDEs Described? 42

The "Out-of-Body Experience" (OBE) 44

Chapter 2: The Haunting Journey of Dr. Bettina Peyton 51

The Perspective of the On-Call Doctor 54

What Are Near-Death Experiences? The Perspective of Scientists 56

Chapter 3: A Doctor's Journey 62

Personal Reflections 65

What Is an Out-of-Body Experience to Medical Science? 67

Chapter 4: Three Journeys Beyond the Border Between Science and Spirituality 72

The First Case Study 72

The Second Case Study 73

The Third Case Study 74

Personal Reflections 74

Chapter 5: A Journey Through the Tunnel: Marianne's Story 77

The Near-Death Experience as an "Alteration of the Sense of Self" 77

Chapter 6: Near-Death Experiences in ICU Survivors: Findings from a Follow-Up Study 82

Study Methods 82

Conclusion 90

Chapter 7: Struck by Fate: A Symphony from the Beyond 93

Chapter 8: A Case of Septic Shock in Obstetrics 102

Chapter 9: Near-Death Experiences and Sleep 109
    Chapter 9: Near-Death Experiences and Sleep 109
    A Case-Control Study on the Relationship Between REM Sleep and Near-Death Experiences 110
Chapter 10: A Systematic Review of Clinical Cases of NDEs 115
Chapter 11: Near-Death Experiences During Cardiac Arrest 120
Chapter 12: Awareness of the Body During Out-of-Body Experiences 124
Chapter 13: Perspectives on the Afterlife Across Cultures and Religions 132
    The Christian View 132
    The Islamic View 134
    The Buddhist View of the Afterlife and Rebirth 136
    The Hindu Perspective on Life, Death, and the Cosmos 137
    The Sikh Perspective on Life, Death, and Spiritual Evolution . 139
    The Jewish Perspective on Life After Death 141
    Beliefs in Other Religions 143
Chapter 14: What Happens to the Body After Death: From Physics to Metaphysics 148
Chapter 15: Subjective Experiences of Contact with the Deceased and Induced After Death Communication (IADC) 155
Conclusions: Personal Reflections and Key Messages 160

Introduction

Near-death experiences (NDEs) have long captivated the collective imagination, offering tantalizing glimpses into possible realms of existence beyond the boundary between life and death. At their core, NDEs are profound, often mystical experiences reported by individuals who have been close to clinical death or have undergone it. Common features of these accounts include "feelings of peace," "out-of-body experiences," "passing through a tunnel," or encounters with deceased loved ones.

The fascination with NDEs is not limited to personal testimonies or academic research; it is also widespread in popular culture. Films such as "Flatliners" (both the original 1990 version and the 2017 remake), "Heaven is for Real," and "The Sixth Sense" explore and dramatize the phenomenon, highlighting the public's strong curiosity and the emotional resonance of stories that push the boundaries of reality. Such cinematic portrayals have further propelled the topic into mainstream discourse, making NDEs as much a dinner table conversation as a subject of rigorous scientific inquiry.

From a scientific perspective, the debate surrounding NDEs is multifaceted. Neuroscientists, psychologists, and other health professionals have long sought to understand the biological and psychological underpinnings of these events.

Is it merely a chemical reaction in our brain as it shuts down? A protective mechanism to shield us from the trauma of death? Or could it suggest something deeper about human consciousness and the nature of our existence?

Scientific research in this field is vibrant, and studies are ongoing. Some research focuses on brain activity, the role of certain neurotransmitters, or the psychological effects on those who have experienced NDEs.

While science seeks empirical explanations, the spiritual and philosophical implications of NDEs ignite intense debate. For many, these experiences, considered "mystical" by some, reaffirm religious beliefs and offer new meaning to the ultimate purpose of their existence.

Near-death experiences, also known by the English term "Near-Death Experiences" (or simply NDE, an acronym I will use throughout the book), actually sit at the intersection of science, spirituality, and storytelling. They challenge our understanding of life, death, and what might lie beyond, making them an ever-fascinating topic for researchers, storytellers, and the general public.

My Perspective on NDEs

As a physician, I have always prioritized understanding the complexities and needs of the human body, diagnosing, treating, and comforting. Throughout my medical career, I have encountered and spoken with many people, and, given my avid curiosity about these topics since my youth (for personal reasons I will not delve into in this book), I have had the opportunity to speak over the years with many individuals, including patients who have faced death.

Their vivid descriptions of otherworldly experiences during moments of extreme physiological stress have produced narratives full of fascination and, at times, disconcerting elements. While my scientific studies have equipped me with the tools to understand some material aspects of death and NDEs, even in light of scientific research on the subject, which I will try to explain as best as possible in this book, these narratives often venture into territories that clinical medicine hesitates to explore.

However, this has further fueled my interest, reinforcing certain personal experiences that I have chosen not to address in this book (to maintain the scientific rigor and objectivity required in the logical reasoning about the subject of this study), but which personally give me confidence in the existence of a different dimension, one we might call "otherworldly," that we may never fully understand in its essence here on Earth.

My experience as a scientific researcher, particularly as the editor-in-chief of several internationally recognized medical-scientific journals, has led me to question the complexity of reality and what should and can be the subject of scientific research. I believe it is impossible to fully explain the complex phenomena we experience daily, often studied by the so-called "soft sciences" such as sociology or psychology, far from the perfection of mathematical sciences, through the principles of physics or mathematical formulas.

Furthermore, not everything can be explained with the tools of science today. Nevertheless, this does not mean that such phenomena are unimportant or should not be the subject of study and research.

The tools used in scientific research are not limited to experiments conducted in laboratories with sophisticated tools and techniques, but can include simple observations or clinical cases (often referred to in medical jargon as "case reports"), which can be equally significant in increasing our knowledge when examined through the lens of the knowledge and experience of those who, as doctors, nurses, or healthcare assistants, work in patient care. Although based on scientific principles and methodologies, this work consists of narratives, relationships with patients, and experiences that often deviate from the cold statistics of scientific studies.

In my view, an interdisciplinary approach drawing from different and sometimes distant sciences like medicine, biology, psychology, and sociology can enhance understanding and study not only of NDEs but of any "complex" phenomenon.

It is well known to scientists, for example, that human feelings and experiences can be very well understood with the tools provided by psychological and sociological sciences, which, although not as perfect as physics and mathematics, are nonetheless scientific disciplines.

Therefore, the reader of this book is forewarned that what is presented here is what has been observed and collected by doctors and published in scientific journals (mainly as clinical cases or "case reports") indexed in important scientific databases, such as Medline, universally recognized not only by doctors and scientists but also by the general public.

Medline is a highly significant bibliographic database in the field of medicine and biomedical sciences. It is managed by the United States National Library of Medicine (NLM) and is part of a larger system called PubMed, which also includes other resources.

Medline collects references and abstracts of scientific articles published in academic journals worldwide, covering a wide range of medical topics, including clinical medicine, biology, life sciences, public health, and many other related disciplines. The database is used by doctors, researchers, students, and healthcare professionals to access scientific studies, clinical cases, and research that contribute to medical practice and the development of scientific knowledge.

Medline is considered one of the primary tools for research in the medical and scientific fields, providing access to up-to-date and authoritative information, essential for evidence-based practice.

Clinical cases, though limited in nature, play a crucial role in hypothesis generation and significantly contribute to what is commonly recognized as "medical science." However, it is important to recognize that even while integrating the knowledge derived from individual clinical cases, we are still far from having a complete and definitive understanding of the entire body of medical knowledge. Each case contributes to building the mosaic of medical science, but the overall picture continues to evolve as new information emerges and old theories are reevaluated.

I would like to conclude with a literary quote that has deeply inspired my research journey. As Shakespeare has Hamlet say: "There are more things in heaven and earth, Horatio, than are dreamt of in your philosophy." This thought constantly reminds me that knowledge is an endless journey and that there is always more to discover than our current understanding can contain. It is curiosity that drives us to look beyond and explore new horizons, fueling the progress of science and knowledge.

The Scientific Method for Studying NDEs

The scientific method is the foundation of modern research: it is a systematic process that allows scientists to test hypotheses and accumulate knowledge objectively and replicably. A scientific study begins with the observation of a phenomenon, followed by the formulation of a hypothesis, the conduction of necessary experiments to test it, and finally, the analysis of data to confirm or refute the original hypothesis under study. The original hypothesis is referred to as the "null hypothesis."

The basic idea is to assume that there is no difference or effect between the groups or variables being studied (hence the term "null"), until proven otherwise (alternative hypothesis). The null hypothesis is useful because it provides a standardized starting point for testing whether the effect observed in the researcher's data is real or likely due to chance. In practice, this helps researchers avoid drawing incorrect conclusions based on possible "random" variations in the data.

In the field of psychology, and specifically in research on near-death experiences, a null hypothesis can be formulated to test, for example, whether a certain variable has a significant impact on the experiences reported by subjects. Suppose a group of researchers wants to examine whether age affects the likelihood of reporting a near-death experience. The null hypothesis might be formulated as follows:

H0: There are no differences in the incidence of near-death experiences between younger and older people.

In this study, researchers will collect data from subjects who have had near-death experiences, recording their age and descriptions of their experiences. They will then analyze whether there are significant differences in the frequency of near-death experiences between the two different age groups after ensuring that the subjects recruited for the study have or have not had near-death experiences in their lifetime. After data collection, specific statistical tests will be conducted to highlight whether differences exist between the two groups; if differences do exist, the tests will reveal whether these differences are statistically significant or merely due to chance.

A crucial aspect of the scientific process is the publication of results, regardless of whether they are positive or negative. It is true, however, that only positive results, those that refute the original hypothesis or "null hypothesis," often find space in publications. However, it would be highly important to publish studies that fail to refute the null hypothesis (which happens rarely), as this would allow scientists to share their findings with the global scientific community. This would facilitate further discussion and investigation, and through more advanced statistical analyses, such as meta-analyses, it could contribute to confirming or revising the initial research results, thereby strengthening the knowledge base on which modern science is founded.

In medicine, in particular, breakthroughs or revolutionary discoveries are built upon a body of evidence generated by dozens, if not hundreds, of scientific studies. These studies, often the result of the brilliant intuition of a few, collectively contribute to advancing the medical field.

PubMed and Medline, databases that collect articles from medical and biomedical journals and make them easily accessible to scientists worldwide, play a crucial role in the field of medical publications. These tools enable researchers to efficiently explore and analyze existing scientific literature, facilitating the conduct of systematic reviews, which, through meta-analyses, are essential for verifying current knowledge, identifying new areas of research, and developing guidelines and consensus documents based on solid scientific evidence.

A systematic review of the literature is a type of research that comprehensively collects and analyzes all available studies and publications on a particular topic up to that point. The goal is to provide a comprehensive overview based on the evidence gathered from all studies conducted on a specific research topic. Below are some key points for those conducting a systematic literature review:

1. **Defining the research question**: The first step in a systematic review is to define a very precise research question. This helps focus the research and identify relevant studies.

2. **Selection criteria**: Clear criteria are established for including studies in the review. These criteria may relate to the type of participants involved, the interventions examined, and the outcomes measured.

3. **Systematic search**: A thorough search is conducted in various databases and sources, not limited to PubMed and Medline, to collect as many relevant studies as possible to the research question.

4. **Analysis**: The collected studies are analyzed to identify common patterns and trends, evaluating the quality and consistency of the results. Often, statistical tests are used in this analysis, such as those employed in meta-analyses.

5. **Synthesis**: The results are then synthesized to draw general conclusions.

Systematic reviews are extremely useful because they reduce the risk of bias, that is, systematic distortions that can influence results. They provide a solid knowledge base on which doctors, researchers, and policymakers can rely to make informed decisions based on the best available scientific evidence.

The content of this book is based on a rigorous review of the available literature on PubMed and Medline. I have analyzed commentaries, letters to the editor, and especially case reports and literature reviews documenting near-death experiences (NDEs). These reports are not merely clinical testimonies but represent pieces of a larger puzzle that helps us explore phenomena at the boundary between medical science and deep human experience.

In this book, I have deliberately not included a review of systematic reviews already published, which will be the subject of an upcoming publication in a scientific journal. Instead, I have chosen to offer a "narrative" review of the state of the art on NDEs, presenting to the reader in a popular form the case reports that have most impressed me and the main systematic reviews found, highlighting the most significant aspects of this fascinating phenomenon.

Scientific Experiments Supporting Near-Death Experiences

Currently, there are no widely accepted scientific experiments that can verify the persistence of human consciousness after death. Although concepts such as the transformation of matter into energy, as described in Einstein's famous equation $E=mc^2$, or some speculative interpretations of quantum mechanics, have sometimes been invoked to explain post-mortem consciousness, there is no direct connection between these physical theories and the survival of consciousness.

Einstein's theory of special relativity establishes that mass and energy are interchangeable according to the equation $E=mc^2$. However, this equation applies to fundamental physical processes involving subatomic particles and energy, not to human consciousness. Consciousness is an emergent phenomenon, the result of complex neurobiological interactions in the brain, and the transformation of brain mass into energy does not imply the preservation or transmission of consciousness itself.

Quantum mechanics, which describes the behavior of subatomic particles, has sometimes been invoked to explain phenomena related to consciousness. Some theorists have speculated that consciousness may have a quantum basis, suggesting that quantum processes in the brain may influence perception and awareness. However, these hypotheses are highly speculative and have not found experimental confirmation. Quantum mechanics applies to extremely small scales, and there is no evidence that these processes can explain the persistence of consciousness after physical death.

Current Scientific Evidence

To date, science does not have the tools or methodologies to demonstrate the survival of consciousness beyond clinical death. Studies on near-death experiences provide data on subjective phenomena experienced by individuals close to death, but these phenomena do not constitute proof of the persistence of consciousness. NDEs can be explained through a combination of neurobiological, psychological, and chemical factors, such as cerebral hypoxia, the release of endorphins, and the activation of specific brain areas.

Current scientific knowledge does not support the idea that consciousness can persist after death through the transformation of matter into energy, as suggested by theories of relativity or quantum mechanics. Human consciousness is considered an emergent phenomenon related to brain activity, and its existence appears to cease with brain death. Research continues to explore the nature of consciousness and near-death experiences, but at present, there is no scientific evidence to confirm the persistence of consciousness beyond physical death.

The main reason for this lack of evidence is that consciousness, which science considers to reside in the brain, cannot be measured or observed with traditional methods once the brain ceases to function.

However, there are scientific studies, published on Medline and recognized by the medical-scientific community, that explore near-death experiences and suggest the possibility of consciousness persisting outside the physical body. These studies, though intriguing, present significant limitations. In particular, they tend to rely on subjective accounts provided by individuals who have experienced life-threatening situations, such as cardiac arrests or other critical clinical conditions. During such events, experiences like seeing a bright light, feeling separated from one's body, or encountering spiritual entities, interpreted as forms of non-physical existence, have often been reported.

One of the most well-known studies in this field is the AWARE study (AWAreness during REsuscitation), conducted by Dr. Sam Parnia and colleagues. This study sought to systematically examine the experiences reported by patients who had suffered cardiac arrest, methodically recording what patients may have seen or heard during the period when they exhibited no measurable vital signs. The goal was to determine whether perceptions of awareness and descriptions of near-death experiences could be somehow verified during documented periods of cardiac or brain activity absence.

The results of these studies, however, have not provided definitive evidence supporting the idea that consciousness persists or that brain matter transforms into conscious energy after death. Most research in this field remains highly speculative and open to multiple interpretations, often influenced by the philosophical or theological assumptions of the researchers or participants.

On the other hand, the growing interest in near-death experiences has led to the emergence of specialized scientific journals, such as the "Journal of Near-Death Experiences," focusing exclusively on this phenomenon. NDEs continue to fascinate dozens of researchers worldwide, stimulating a scientific and philosophical debate that is still evolving.

Maintaining a rational perspective does not mean, however, excluding the possibility that consciousness may survive death and that life after death may exist. As suggested in Stéphane Allix's book *The Test: Incredible Proof of the Afterlife* (Skyhorse, 2018), these phenomena deserve to be investigated with an open mind, free from preconceptions or prejudices. Allix, a journalist and author, recounts in his book fifteen years of investigations in which he gathered experiences and testimonies that led him to admit that life after death is a "reality, a scientific and rational hypothesis based on facts."

Allix explores a new line of study emerging within psychiatry, focused on contacts with the deceased. This new discipline aims to scientifically examine the testimonies of people who claim to have communicated with their deceased loved ones. These contacts, which often occur in therapy settings or through mediums, are now being analyzed with scientific tools to assess their authenticity and psychological impact. Although the field is still in its early stages, growing academic interest suggests that the exploration of post-mortem consciousness may one day reveal aspects of reality that currently elude our understanding.

Ultimately, as *The Test: Incredible Proof of the Afterlife* suggests, a rational and scientific approach can and should coexist with openness to new possibilities. The mystery of consciousness and life after death remains largely unexplored territory, and the progress of science depends on our ability to investigate without prejudice, leaving the door open to discoveries.

Another book I highly recommend reading is one written by an anesthesiologist, Dr. Eben Alexander, who experienced an extraordinary event. Struck by severe bacterial meningitis, a condition so grave that almost no one survives, Dr. Alexander fell into a coma for a week. During this period, spent in a state of complete unconsciousness from a medical point of view, he reported incredible experiences of a place he describes as the afterlife.

In his 2012 bestseller *Proof of Heaven* (Windsor, 2013), Alexander does not simply recount his experience but also provides scientific arguments to support the existence of a reality beyond death. With the rigor of a physician and the authenticity of someone who has personally experienced a near-death experience, Dr. Alexander explains why his visions cannot be easily dismissed as hallucinations or products of a brain in agony. He details the journey he undertook during that week of coma, a journey that, according to him, proves that consciousness can exist independently of the physical body.

The strength of Alexander's book lies not only in his personal account but also in how he integrates his experience with scientific knowledge. He challenges traditional neurobiological explanations and offers a new perspective on the possibility that consciousness may survive death. This book represents an important contribution to the debate on what might happen after death and deserves to be read by anyone interested in exploring these mysteries with an open and critical mind.

Along with *The Test: Incredible Proof of the Afterlife* by Stéphane Allix, Dr. Eben Alexander's book enriches the discussion on a topic that, while remaining deeply enigmatic, continues to fascinate and challenge our current understandings of life, death, and consciousness. Both books offer perspectives that, although not definitive, contribute to a fundamental debate and invite us to consider the possibility that reality is far more complex than we are accustomed to thinking.

The Challenges of Scientifically Approaching the Study of Near-Death Experiences

The subject of NDEs remains a field of great interest for both the scientific community and the general public, but the methodological and ethical challenges in exploring this phenomenon are significant. Let's examine some of them.

Methodological Challenges

Measuring or quantifying consciousness, especially in situations of cardiac arrest or clinical death, is complex. NDEs are, by nature, highly subjective and non-reproducible experiences. This makes it difficult to apply the standard scientific method, which, as described earlier, relies on observation, repeatability, and control. Additionally, patients' memories can be influenced by various confounding factors such as medications, stress, and different neurological conditions during and after the critical event.

Ethical Challenges

Conducting experiments involving clinical death or similar situations carries considerable ethical dilemmas. It would require monitoring patients in potentially terminal states, raising questions about patient autonomy, informed consent, and the morality of conducting such experiments in particularly delicate circumstances. The safety and well-being of patients must always be prioritized, which limits the nature and scope of research that can be conducted with ethical authorization from scientific committees.

Scientists who have attempted to explore the concept of post-mortem consciousness through the prism of quantum physics, proposing theories that consider consciousness as a quantum phenomenon that could exist independently of the brain, have faced harsh criticism, as their theories, much like psychoanalytic studies, remain largely speculative and not accepted by the mainstream scientific community.

Recently, research on consciousness and advanced brain functions has benefited from imaging technologies such as functional magnetic resonance imaging (fMRI) and electroencephalography (EEG). These highly advanced tools, used for diagnosing neurological system diseases, allow for the study of brain activity in a non-invasive manner and in real-time, offering new avenues for understanding how the brain manages experiences felt by consciousness.

So far, science has not been able to definitively confirm or refute the idea that consciousness may survive the death of the physical body in some energetic or quantum form. However, research on near-death experiences (NDEs) is a rapidly evolving field, fueled by advances in resuscitation techniques and the increase in testimonies about these experiences. These developments have allowed progress in understanding NDEs, although the nature of the consciousness associated with such experiences remains largely mysterious and subject to personal and cultural interpretations.

Scientific research on NDEs challenges our current concepts of consciousness and its relationship with brain functioning. Scholars like Martial, in his 2020 scientific research (the freely downloadable version from PubMed/Medline is available at: https://pubmed.ncbi.nlm.nih.gov/31982302/), suggest that to better understand the NDE phenomenon, a new theoretical approach distinguishing between vigilance, connection, and internal awareness is necessary. This framework could offer greater methodological and conceptual clarity, allowing NDEs to be linked to other related phenomena, fostering a more precise and detailed understanding of near-death experiences.

Indeed, forty-five years ago, the first evidence of a near-death experience during a comatose state paved the way for a new paradigm in studying the neural basis of consciousness in non-responsive states. While in common vision, consciousness is thought to disappear with a coma at the cessation of brain activity, this is an overly simplistic interpretation. Scholars argue that a new conceptual framework distinguishing between internal awareness, wakefulness, and connection is essential to understanding the NDE phenomenon.

As science continues to advance, new theories or evidence may emerge that shed light on the nature of consciousness and NDEs. For now, the persistence of consciousness after death remains one of the great unresolved questions of human existence. However, thanks to new approaches and advances in consciousness studies, the NDE phenomenon may become increasingly understandable, opening new research directions not only on near-death experiences but also on the science of consciousness in general.

The Purpose of This Book

This book aims to explore a complex topic already addressed by other authors but examined here through a lens of analysis that I believe is new and original. My goal is not merely to gather what is already known about the NDE phenomenon (or near-death experiences) to present it to an audience of enthusiasts or skeptics. Instead, I aim to adopt a critical approach, scientifically analyzing the discoveries and observations that doctors and researchers have published over years of experiments and studies.

I firmly believe that a scientific perspective, open but not prejudiced, offers the best outlook for trying to bridge the gap between empirical evidence and the testimonies of those who have experienced these extraordinary events. I do not delve into this subject to provide definitive answers but to stimulate reflection, bring to light narratives often overlooked in medical discussions, and explore the fascinating combination of physiological explanations and the profound mysteries of human consciousness.

My intent is to present the stories told by scientists, without neglecting the human and spiritual implications these experiences entail, with the utmost respect, openness, and a genuine desire for understanding. I have sought to blend science and, to a lesser extent, storytelling to offer readers a unique and engaging perspective.

The stories recounted in this book are absolutely true, drawn and inspired by real cases published in scientific journals by doctors and neuroscientists. Scientific references are cited in each chapter, allowing curious and knowledgeable readers to further explore each case.

In this first edition, my research has focused on PubMed and Medline, the primary resources used by scientists and researchers worldwide. I have maintained the original bibliographic citations so that readers can continue their journey of discovery, trying to build their own truth on such a complex and controversial topic.

I wish you an enjoyable read and a stimulating adventure in this fascinating journey through science and human consciousness.

Chapter 1: Between Life and Death: What Does Science Say?

Everything was shrouded in darkness and silence, except for a distant glow that seemed to beckon her. Elena, thirty-five years old and a mother, lay motionless on the cold hospital bed, surrounded by the intermittent sounds of machines and the constant movement of medical staff. A sudden cardiac arrest had torn her from her daily routine, catapulting her into an unknown place. While the doctors desperately fought to save her, Elena was drawn toward that light, which promised a mysterious comfort.

"I felt like I was floating towards a warm, welcoming light, where every fear and worry melted away like snow in the sun," Elena would later recount, her voice trembling but clear. "It was more than just peace; it was a feeling of universal love, something I had never experienced before."

Elena's case is not an exception. Around the world, thousands of people have shared similar experiences—episodes where they brushed against the boundary between life and death and returned to tell what they had seen. These Near-Death Experiences, commonly known as "NDEs," are not merely anecdotal but have sparked serious investigation among scientists and researchers into what happens in our brains and consciousness during those critical moments.

This chapter, and indeed this book, will explore NDEs from a scientific perspective, aiming to unravel the complex relationship between neurology, psychology, and the personal testimonies of those who have gone through these profound moments of crisis. As we proceed with this exploration, we will examine not only what these experiences reveal about death but also what they tell us about how we live, what we value in life, and how we interpret existence itself.

The concept of life after death has always piqued human interest, generating countless stories, beliefs, and spiritual doctrines since ancient times. NDEs are not just anecdotal; they have become a subject of study, drawing scientists into an increasingly heated scientific debate. NDE episodes are characterized by intense psychological and sensory events in which individuals, on the brink of death, report sensations of deep peace, encounters with bright lights, out-of-body perceptions, and sometimes mysterious adventures in a completely different realm or dimension (Greyson, 2000a; Greyson, 1983; Charland-Verville et al., 2014).

How widespread are these experiences? Prevalence of the Phenomenon and Differences Between NDEs and "NDE-like" Experiences

Contrary to what one might imagine, the prevalence of NDEs in scientific studies conducted globally is surprisingly high. Some research indicates that between 6% and 23% of survivors of cardiac arrest—people who have suffered severe heart dysfunction due to heart attacks or other causes—reported experiencing such events (Parnia et al., 2001; Schwaninger et al., 2002). This statistic underscores the importance of the phenomenon and raises questions about its nature and implications.

The phenomenon of NDEs becomes even more fascinating when we consider the so-called "NDE-like" experiences, lived by individuals who were not in imminent life-threatening situations. These people describe sensations similar to those of NDEs during deep meditation sessions or following episodes of fainting, medically known as "syncope." What makes these experiences particularly intriguing is the fact that some NDE-like experiences have even been reproduced in experimental laboratory settings, suggesting that such phenomena may not necessarily be linked to the proximity of death (Lempert et al., 1994; Beauregard et al., 2009).

These findings have led some scientists to hypothesize that NDEs may represent brain response to a variety of extreme stimuli rather than being exclusively tied to imminent death. In other words, the NDE phenomenon could reflect neurobiological mechanisms that are activated not only in life-threatening conditions but also in situations where consciousness is significantly altered.

This significantly broadens the scope of research on NDEs, encouraging scholars to explore not only the medical circumstances in which these experiences occur but also the neurological and psychological processes that may underlie such phenomena. For example, laboratory studies that have induced NDE-like experiences through brain stimulation or controlled hypoxia suggest that specific areas of the brain may be involved in the genesis of these experiences.

Definition and Causes of NDEs

There is no universally accepted scientific definition of "near-death experience" (NDE), nor have definitive causes for these experiences been identified. It is crucial to distinguish between the concept of "cause" and that of "association" in scientific research. Not all associations (or correlations) between two phenomena imply a direct causal relationship. For causality to be established, a cause must precede the effect and directly generate it. However, two variables can be associated without there being evidence that one is the cause of the other.

Numerous hypotheses have been proposed to explain NDEs, ranging from psychological coping mechanisms to complex neural processes. Psychological mechanisms interpret NDEs as adaptation strategies to situations of extreme stress or proximity to death. Neurologically, NDEs have been associated with specific alterations in brain activity, as evidenced by changes in brain waves or the effects of neurochemical substances under critical conditions.

Studies such as that of Timmermann and collaborators (2018) have explored the correlations between NDEs and brain activity in controlled experiments. This study found that the administration of DMT (N,N-Dimethyltryptamine) induces experiences with phenomenological characteristics very similar to NDEs, including feelings of transcendence, communication with entities, and the perception of another reality. DMT, a powerful psychedelic substance found in certain plants, is known to induce profound alterations in consciousness, often described as visions. It is also used in ritual and religious contexts, such as in the preparation of ayahuasca, a traditional Amazonian beverage.

These findings suggest that DMT could be used to model NDEs in a laboratory setting, allowing for systematic study of these experiences. Furthermore, scientific research has attributed NDEs to the effects of other pharmacological substances, such as ketamine, a dissociative anesthetic known to induce altered states of consciousness. Ketamine acts on NMDA (N-methyl-D-aspartate) receptors in the brain, which are crucial for synaptic plasticity, learning, and memory. The effects of ketamine include out-of-body experiences, sensations of transcendence, and alterations in the perception of time and space, similar to those reported during NDEs.

A 2015 study explored the relationships between ketamine use and near-death experiences, finding that 79.6% of participants reported experiences similar to NDEs. This study concluded that ketamine can reliably induce experiences that mimic NDEs, suggesting that such experiences may be explained, at least in part, by neurochemical alterations and brain activity under conditions of extreme stress or proximity to death (Jansen, 1997).

In summary, while the causes of NDEs remain a topic of debate, correlations with neurochemical alterations and brain processes offer a promising perspective for better understanding these complex phenomena. Continuing to explore these mechanisms may bring us closer to a more complete understanding of NDEs and their significance in the context of human consciousness.

Medical Conditions Associated with NDEs

Near-death experiences (NDEs) can manifest in a wide range of clinical settings. Van Lommel and collaborators (2001; 2017) identified NDEs in various critical medical scenarios, including cardiac arrest caused by a myocardial infarction, which is one of the most common circumstances. Other medical conditions associated with NDEs include postpartum hemorrhagic shock or those due to surgical complications, septic or anaphylactic shock, and cardiac arrest resulting from electrocution.

Extreme situations such as coma from head trauma, cerebral hemorrhages, suicide attempts, and accidents with a risk of drowning or suffocation are also associated with the onset of an NDE. Even episodes of severe apnea, where the flow of oxygen to the brain is temporarily interrupted, can trigger an NDE, which tends to manifest in contexts where the threat to life is palpable and imminent.

NDEs have been observed in various pathological states where cardiac and respiratory function is compromised, suggesting a possible link between the malfunction of these vital systems and the perception of experiences at the edge of life. These experiences offer a unique perspective on the extreme reactions of the human body and the possible interactions between mind and body under conditions of severe physical stress.

Scientific research continues to explore not only the triggering causes of NDEs but also the long-term implications of such experiences on the well-being of those who survive a critical event. Particular attention is given to the changes that may occur in the way one views life and death, as well as the possible neurobiological explanations underlying these profound experiences.

In the rest of this book, we will delve into the consequences of NDEs for those who have experienced them, including the psychological, spiritual, and philosophical transformations that often follow such experiences. We will also examine how these experiences influence the long-term well-being of survivors, exploring their new perspectives on life and death. NDEs, with their potential to redefine our relationship with existence and mortality, represent a fascinating field of study that requires an integrated approach, capable of combining scientific discoveries with the depth of human experience.

NDEs and Self-Defining Memories (SDM)

Near-death experiences (NDEs) leave an indelible mark on the memory of those who experience them, often becoming "self-defining memories" (SDM), according to psychologists. SDMs are crucial in the formation of personal identity, as they connect the different phases of the self—past, present, and future—and contribute to the construction of a coherent narrative of one's life (Blagov et al., 2004). In this sense, NDEs are not merely extraordinary events but experiences that deeply root themselves in consciousness, becoming an integral part of one's self-perception.

In the book, *Proof of Heaven* (Alexander, 2013), neurologist Eben Alexander recounts his own NDE, experienced after falling into a coma due to severe meningitis and miraculously returning to life. Dr. Alexander describes how the memories of the otherworldly realm he visited remained indelibly imprinted in his mind, profoundly influencing his life and worldview.

SDMs are memories of significant moments that play a fundamental role in defining our identity. These are not just past events but experiences that have profoundly shaped our perception of ourselves. These memories include moments of intense joy, significant challenges, successes, or failures that have left an indelible mark on our consciousness.

SDMs connect our past with the present and shape our expectations for the future, influencing daily decisions and behavior. They form the narrative fabric through which we interpret who we are, how we perceive ourselves, and how we present ourselves to others. They serve as internal reference points, guiding our actions and helping us decipher new experiences.

Scholars examine the specificity of SDMs, the personal details that emerge, recurring themes, and the emotional response evoked during their recollection (Blagov et al., 2004). These memories are particularly relevant in the context of NDEs, events filled with intense emotion and cognition, capable of radically transforming an individual's life perspective.

NDEs, therefore, can become self-defining memories that introduce new understandings and change a person's concept of self. A near-death experience, with its profound moments of serenity, visions, or perceived encounters with otherworldly entities, can determinately and lastingly influence how the individual views the world, interprets life and death, and relates to others.

NDEs not only enrich an individual's narrative but can also alter fundamental aspects of life, such as the perception of death, the priorities in values and goals, and the commitment to personal relationships. In this way, NDEs deeply integrate into the psyche of the survivor, contributing to the redefinition of their identity and existential path.

From Psychology to Spirituality

Scholars analyze NDEs through the lens of self-defining memories to understand how such experiences influence the formation of memories, highlighting significant personal insights, recurring themes like spirituality or reconciliation with the past, and the intense emotional reactions that result. These elements help to understand how NDEs can act as catalysts for deep reflection and self-reconstruction, offering new perspectives on one's life and experiences.

In this way, NDEs transcend their nature as merely clinical or neurological phenomena, emerging as crucial moments of personal growth and identity development. They reveal the powerful connection between extreme human experiences and self-construction through the memories that define who we are.

Recognizing the therapeutic value of these memories, particularly their positive manifestations, can be fundamental for the mental well-being of individuals. This is especially true for significant experiences like NDEs, emphasizing the need to understand, integrate, and give meaning to them (Cassol et al., 2019).

This creates an intriguing dialogue between science and the almost mystical realm of NDEs, stimulating reflection on what these experiences can reveal about our consciousness, existence, and daily reality.

In this context, the transition from psychological to mystical-spiritual issues takes on particular importance. Many individuals who have experienced an NDE report encounters with figures perceived as divine or spiritual and a profound sense of unity with the universe. These experiences often lead to radical changes in how they perceive the world, with an increase in their spirituality and a significant transformation in their daily lives.

The encounters that occur during an NDE can reinforce, modify, or even give rise to new religious or spiritual beliefs, leading people to reconsider their value system and the meaning of their existence.

Understanding NDEs thus offers a unique opportunity to explore the boundary between science and spirituality, challenging scholars to integrate multidisciplinary approaches that include psychology, neuroscience, religion, and philosophy. The mystical encounters that occur during an NDE, often described as moments of profound peace and unconditional love, raise fundamental questions about the essence of consciousness and the possible existence of non-corporeal dimensions not yet fully understood by modern science.

Analyzing how NDEs influence people's religious and spiritual beliefs can enrich the debate on the implications of these experiences, not only for those who have lived through them but also for the scientific and spiritual community in general. This dialogue opens new avenues for understanding how human resilience confronts the mystery of death and the eternal question of the afterlife, providing a unique window into the deep human desire to find coherence and meaning in one's existence. Knowing that there is a happy and eternal life beyond the very short one lived on the physical plane we all know can be a source of comfort in the face of grief and loss.

These observations support the adoption of a multidisciplinary approach to the study of NDEs, integrating neuroscience, psychology, medicine, and humanities such as philosophy and theology. Such an integrated approach can significantly enrich our understanding of NDEs, reflecting their complex and multidimensional nature.

A multidisciplinary approach allows for a deeper understanding of NDEs: integrating medical knowledge with psychological and spiritual insights can provide holistic and more effective care for patients who have experienced or are living through critical moments, who have been close to death, as well as for their loved ones who care for them or experience the pain and proximity to death.

What Happens After an NDE?

As previously mentioned, the repercussions of Near-Death Experiences (NDEs) on individuals who have lived through them can often be profoundly transformative. Many of those who have experienced an NDE report significant changes in how they view the world and their own personality. Typically, there is an increase in compassion for others and less focus on materialistic aspirations (Greyson, 1997; Ring, 1984; Van Lommel et al., 2001).

Many studies have documented the positive consequences of NDEs, including a life characterized by greater altruism, spiritual growth, and a deeper search for the meaning of life. Other effects include a decrease in attachment to materialistic values and less fear of death (Noyes, 1980; Groth-Marnat et al., 1998; Knoblauch et al., 2001; Parnia et al., 2001; Moody, 2005; Khanna et al., 2014).

However, the subjective nature of NDEs and the absence of a defined interpretive framework mean that the understanding and description of such experiences are influenced by multiple individual, cultural, and religious factors (Van Lommel et al., 2017).

It has been observed that near-death experiences can vary significantly depending on the cultural and religious context of survivors, tending to reflect and reinforce the individual's pre-existing beliefs (Parnia, 2017).

Although early research on NDEs tended to focus on emotionally positive experiences (Ring, 1980; 1984), more recent studies recognize a broader range of emotional responses and long-term impacts on those who have had an NDE.

The emotional responses and long-term impact of NDEs are highly variable and can include both positive and negative reactions, although the former usually prevails.

Among the negative effects, some individuals report experiencing greater difficulty adapting to everyday life, which can be understandable after such a deeply transformative and highly traumatic experience for the individual.

Some NDE survivors describe feelings of isolation and loneliness, resulting from the difficulty of sharing such an exceptional and personal experience with others who may not understand or may harbor skepticism. Additionally, the intense spiritual experiences lived during an NDE can also provoke internal conflicts, especially if they contrast with the religious or philosophical beliefs the individual had before experiencing the NDE.

Among the psychological effects that can be considered positive, NDEs can lead to a renewed sense of vocation and the redefinition of life priorities. However, such a change can also cause tensions in personal and professional relationships, as the individual may feel compelled to radically change their lifestyle and goals. From a behavioral point of view, it is not uncommon for those who have experienced an NDE to embark on new careers, particularly in fields related to helping and caring for others, or to engage in volunteer and charitable activities, seeking to give deeper meaning to their existence.

Scientific studies continue to delve into the study of these changes, especially in emotional and behavioral responses, examining how different cultural and personal contexts can influence and condition the processing of an NDE.

In particular, research is focusing on how coping strategies and community support can help individuals positively integrate an

NDE into their daily lives, promoting healthier adaptation and a deeper personal and collective understanding of these extraordinary phenomena.

Impact of NDEs on Doctors, Patients, Families, and Caregivers

Near-death Experiences (NDEs) present significant challenges in their understanding and management, but they can also have a very positive influence, particularly for those who work in helping professions or work closely with others. For example, having lived through an NDE has often positively transformed the interaction between doctor and patient, improving the quality of the therapeutic relationship (Greyson, 2015).

Mental health professionals, in particular, have used NDE studies to address and reduce suicidal thoughts in their patients, facilitate grief recovery, and decrease the incidence of post-traumatic stress disorder (Greyson, 2015). This approach has emphasized the importance of considering the emotional and spiritual needs, especially in some categories of patients, such as the terminally ill, promoting a more empathetic and deeper relationship between doctor and patient. As a result, there has been an improvement in the therapeutic alliance and compliance, with a positive impact on treatment effectiveness.

On the other hand, patients who have experienced an NDE often describe undergoing a profound spiritual and emotional transformation. Many of them report having found a new sense of life, becoming more existentially aware, and having lived through mystical experiences that have enriched their life perspective (Khanna et al., 2015).

These changes have often led to greater serenity, acceptance, and inner peace, positively influencing the patient's overall well-being. The described transformations often extend to the patient's family and friends, who, in various studies, have reported an increased sense of comfort, hope, and inspiration, finding solace in the prospect of an existence that transcends physical life (Greyson, 2015). This new perspective has facilitated grief management and helped strengthen family cohesion and interpersonal relationships.

NDEs challenge traditional interpretations of science and medicine, raising profound questions about the nature of consciousness and existence. This requires health professionals to adopt a holistic approach to the human experience, integrating both the material and immaterial aspects of life.

In this context, in an article published in 2016 in the Journal of Health and Social Sciences, I proposed a redefinition of health in a global and holistic sense, compared to the definition given by the World Health Organization. I suggested including spiritual well-being alongside physical, psychological, and social well-being, emphasizing the need to recognize and address people's spiritual needs to promote truly integrated and "holistic" health (Chirico, 2016).

End-of-Life Contact with Deceased Loved Ones

Experiences of contact with the deceased, also known as End-of-Life Dreams and Visions (ELDVs), are phenomena frequently reported by terminally ill patients, especially in palliative care and hospice settings. These experiences can occur during sleep or in a waking state and often involve visions of deceased loved ones, religious figures, or spiritual entities. Unlike hallucinations related to delirium, ELDVs are generally perceived as comforting and meaningful, helping to reduce the fear of death and facilitating the transition of the dying toward death (Hession et al., 2022).

According to a systematic review conducted by Rabitti et al. (2024), about 50-60% of hospice patients (terminal patients) report having these experiences. However, ELDVs are often at risk of being misclassified as delirium or pathological hallucinations, especially in a care context that adopts a strictly biomedical approach. This can lead to an underestimation of their significance for the patient, thus depriving the patient of an important space for expression and communication.

Studies indicate that ELDVs have a profound emotional impact on patients, influencing their existential well-being and facilitating preparation for death. The visions and dreams described by patients include encounters with deceased loved ones, journeys to familiar or transcendent places, and, in some cases, the presence of spiritual or divine figures. These experiences are often accompanied by a strong emotional charge, which can be positive, with a sense of peace and acceptance, or, in some cases, negative, especially when linked to unresolved traumatic events (Rabitti et al., 2024).

ELDVs offer a unique perspective on the dying process, suggesting that such experiences may play a fundamental role in the meaning patients attribute to their existence and their approach to end-of-life. Fenwick and Brayne (2007) propose that these experiences may represent moments of great spiritual value, stemming from the innate desire for connection and communication that characterizes the human being.

From a medical-scientific perspective, in clinical settings, recognizing and valuing ELDVs can enrich the therapeutic relationship, offering health professionals a greater understanding of patients' spiritual and emotional needs. Training healthcare workers to recognize and support these experiences is therefore crucial, as suggested by recent studies highlighting the need for a holistic approach to end-of-life care (Rabitti et al., 2024).

From Naturalism to a Holistic Dimension of Medicine

Naturalism has exerted considerable influence on the academic and cultural landscape of the West, particularly in the fields of medicine and science. With roots stretching back to the ancient Greeks, naturalism considers the interactions and properties of atoms as explanatory keys for every aspect of the world and human experience (Halverson, 1976).

Philosopher W. T. Jones interpreted the world, according to naturalism, as a vast machine, where every event is describable through the properties and relationships of material particles.

During the Enlightenment, an era of scientific and political revolutions, naturalism gained ground and, with the advancement of science, became the dominant paradigm in medicine (Halverson, 1976). Traditionally, medical practice has focused on diagnosing and treating diseases based primarily on physical symptoms, often neglecting the psychological, social, and spiritual aspects of patients (Engel, 1992).

In the 20th century, however, a more comprehensive medical paradigm emerged, defined as "holistic," which considers the human person as an interconnected entity rather than merely a mechanism governed by physical laws (De Angulo et al., 2010). This approach has facilitated a deeper understanding of the environmental and social interactions that influence an individual's health and disease.

Dr. George L. Engel criticized the previous Enlightenment model for its reductionist approach, in which scientists, considering themselves objective observers, perceived nature as something external and unaffected by their observations. This viewpoint limited doctors to the role of mere technicians of bodily processes, ignoring the human aspects of their patients.

Today, reality is considered subjective and is defined by the perception of those who experience it. As the German philosopher Immanuel Kant stated, "Reality as we know it is the product of our mind." The famous physicist Albert Einstein also emphasized that "Reality is merely an illusion, albeit a very persistent one." These quotes reflect the idea that individual perception plays a crucial role in the construction of reality, a concept that has profoundly influenced modern medicine, promoting a more holistic and patient-centered approach.

In contemporary times, the shift in the medical paradigm is part of a broader academic movement that David Brooks has described in the New York Times as "neural Buddhism." This current of thought does not lead to militant atheism but rather to a synthesis between science and mysticism, with significant potential cultural impacts (Brooks, 2008).

NDEs emerge in this context as a notable medical development that fosters better patient health and promotes an understanding of consciousness that goes beyond naturalistic theories (Kopel, 2019). These developments suggest a growing acceptance of the complex dimensions of human experience, emphasizing, as mentioned earlier, the importance of an approach that integrates physical, psychological, social, and spiritual well-being.

Healthcare professionals, particularly nurses and doctors, need to be knowledgeable about the elements of NDEs and more aware of the most appropriate and relevant interventions. This knowledge can be important in inducing positive and "adequate" reactions in patients who "return" from an NDE episode.

Scientific Interpretations of Near-Death Experiences (NDEs)

Near-death experiences (NDEs) have sparked great interest and have been studied by various scientific groups. These groups primarily include neuroscientists, but also theologians, Christologists, and parapsychologists. The PubMed database, for example, contains over 538,500 articles that comment on and investigate the phenomenon of NDEs (Habek et al., 2022).

According to some theological and spiritual theories, consciousness can separate from the brain's neural substrate. Psychological theories, on the other hand, interpret NDEs as a dissociative defense mechanism that manifests in situations of extreme danger or as a reflection of birth memories. Organic theories, on the other hand, base NDEs on phenomena such as cerebral hypoxia, anoxia, hypercapnia, and biochemical alterations of brain neurotransmitters (French 2005, Parnia et al, 2007; Charland-Verville et al, 2014; Bourdin et al, 2017; Cassol et al, 2019).

NDEs occur in about 17% of people who are near death, whether they are children or the elderly, people with comorbidities (affected by pathologies) or healthy, believers or atheists, and regardless of profession or level of education (Long, 2014).

Timmerman and collaborators discuss the biochemistry of NDEs and their association with the psychedelic phenomenology conditioned by the release of dimethyltryptamine during the dying process, citing Strassman (Timmermann et al, 2018; Strassman, 2001).

Even NDE scales with 80 variables have been developed and are used to evaluate the organic or psychological origin of an NDE in the patient (Greyson, 1983). Recently, some researchers have developed and validated a psychometric tool for the evaluation and measurement of NDEs (Martial et al, 2020).

A Critical Reflection on Near-Death Experiences: Between Neurobiology and Psychological Theories

Near-death experiences (NDEs) represent a complex and fascinating phenomenon that challenges current scientific understandings of consciousness and perception. During NDEs, the subject's heartbeat and breathing temporarily cease, accompanied by the absence of detectable brain waves on an electroencephalogram (EEG) and a lack of auditory brainstem responses. Despite this suspension of vital functions, subjects report a series of intense and structured subjective experiences, commonly including episodes of separation from the physical body (out-of-body experiences, OBE), passage through a dark tunnel, encounters with bright lights, deceased loved ones, spirit guides or mystical beings, and the perception of a boundary not to be crossed (Greyson, 2000; van Lommel et al., 2001; French, 2005; Parnia et al., 2007).

While NDEs share similar characteristics worldwide, regardless of language, culture, or age, they can be explained through various scientific hypotheses. Among these, dysfunctions of the temporal lobe, imbalances of neurotransmitters such as glutamate and serotonin, and electrolyte disturbances during physical crises stand out (Carr, 1981; Persinger and Makarec, 1987; Blackmore and Troscianko, 1988; Appelby, 1989). Other theories suggest that NDEs may result from intrusions of REM sleep or cerebral hypoxia, conditions that can produce visual phenomena and out-of-body sensations. Additionally, it has been hypothesized that electrical stimulation of specific brain areas, such as the angular gyrus, may induce experiences similar to NDEs (Blanke et al., 2002).

An interesting aspect of NDEs is the perception of bright lights, which could be explained by the production of biophotons in the brain. These biophotons, generated during bioluminescent radical reactions, could be perceived as phosphenes, or visual sensations in the absence of external stimuli, and may contribute to the formation of the luminous images often described during NDEs (Bókkon and Salari, 2012). This phenomenon is supported by studies showing increased biophoton production during and after states of cerebral hypoxia (Imaizumi et al., 1984; Suzuki et al., 1985).

Despite these neurobiological and psychological explanations, NDEs remain a phenomenon that cannot be fully understood through current scientific theories alone. Some features, such as OBEs and the perception of external events while the subject is unconscious, challenge conventional medical science interpretations and suggest the need for further interdisciplinary research that integrates neuroscience, quantum physics, and consciousness studies.

It is essential to understand that, while science has made progress in understanding NDEs, many questions remain unanswered, suggesting that these experiences may require new paradigms to be fully understood. As Facco and Agrillo (2012a) stated, it is time to overcome cultural prejudices and include consciousness and spirituality in neuroscience from a free and secular scientific perspective.

The Materialist and Spiritual Views of NDEs

The organic theories that seek to explain Near-Death Experiences (NDEs) through neurobiological mechanisms do not necessarily contradict the spiritualist view that consciousness can exist outside the body, embodied in the soul. On the contrary, they could be seen as complementary.

Neurobiological explanations, such as the hypothesis of biophoton emission or residual brain activity during anoxia states, describe what happens in the brain during an NDE from a physiological perspective. However, these theories do not rule out the possibility that consciousness can exist independently of the physical body. The persistence of brain activity in moments when the person is presumed to be clinically dead could be interpreted as a bridge between the physical and spiritual worlds.

According to this view, NDEs could represent a transition or interaction between physical consciousness and a spiritual dimension. The phenomena observed in the brain could be physical manifestations of a process involving a consciousness not bound by material limits but using the body as a temporary means of expression. In this sense, neurobiological theories do not exclude the possibility of the soul's existence; rather, they could provide a partial explanation, limited by the current scientific perspective.

Personally, I believe that the interaction between science and spirituality is a fascinating and still largely unexplored field. While science seeks to understand the physical mechanisms underlying human experiences, spiritual views offer a perspective that goes beyond the tangible, opening the door to possibilities that science alone may not be able to fully explain. The balance between these two perspectives could bring us closer to a more integrated understanding of consciousness and existence itself.

How Are NDEs Described?

According to Hashemi and collaborators (2023), the foundations and contents of Near-Death Experiences (NDEs) reported by individuals from various cultures show remarkable similarities, while differences mainly emerge in the interpretations and explanations of such experiences. Among all the reported NDEs, there is a common core that includes elements such as out-of-body experiences, passage through a tunnel, and heightened senses. This core is universally recognized and transcends ethnic, geographical, religious, and cultural barriers, manifesting independently of local beliefs and traditions.

Beyond this central core, a series of more specific experiences, deeply rooted in the personal archive of the NDE experiencer, occurs. These include symbols, images, and characters significant only to the individual in question, suggesting a cultural and personal component in the interpretations of NDEs. It is evident that, while some aspects of near-death experiences are influenced by culture, others are universal. The most critical and cross-cultural features include altered states of consciousness and anomalous perceptions, which manifest in all the cultures examined.

However, some characteristics of NDEs vary significantly depending on the cultural context. For example, in some cultures, the presence of specific religious figures is reported, while in others, encounters with deceased relatives predominate. Additionally, the pattern of experiences varies: individuals from certain cultures may describe an out-of-body experience, passage through a tunnel, and a life review, while in other cultures, these elements are less present or absent. These differences suggest that the perception of NDEs is significantly influenced by individuals' cultural backgrounds.

In the research by Hashemi and collaborators (2023), four main categories of NDEs were identified through a systematic review of cases reported in the literature: supernatural, spiritual and religious, cognitive, and emotional experiences.

Supernatural experiences, the most frequently reported category, include subcategories such as out-of-body experiences (OBE) and metaphysical perceptions, including passage through a tunnel, seeing one's body from above, and telepathy. In particular, out-of-body experiences, described by the majority of such types of NDEs, represent a crucial element of these experiences. However, the frequency and form of such experiences vary: for example, passage through a tunnel is commonly reported in Indian and Buddhist NDEs, but less frequently in Thai NDEs (Greyson, 2015; Murphy, 2001).

Spiritual and religious experiences include encounters with religious figures and deceased loved ones and feelings of unity with the universe, while cognitive experiences include life reviews, the perception of specific knowledge, and the loss of a sense of time.

Emotional experiences are divided into positive, characterized by a profound sense of peace, and negative, which include visions of hellish scenarios, although the latter is less common (Cassol et al., 2019).

Research conducted in this field, showing a stable pattern of enhanced consciousness and heightened senses, leads, according to Hashemi and colleagues (2023), to the "clarity of NDEs," suggesting that such experiences may represent a more concrete and tangible reality than everyday reality. Nevertheless, this phenomenon remains, according to Hashemi and colleagues, "medically inexplicable."

The "Out-of-Body Experience" (OBE)

"Supernatural experiences" represent one of the most fascinating and controversial categories of experiences related to Near-Death Experiences (NDEs). Within this broad spectrum of phenomena, "Out-of-Body Experiences" (OBE) occupy a central place. These experiences are mainly divided into two subcategories: true "out-of-body" experiences and "supernatural and metaphysical perceptions." The latter include phenomena such as passage through a tunnel, movement towards the ceiling, seeing one's physical body from above (autoscopy), awareness of distant locations, the ability to pass through solid objects like walls (self-permeability), simultaneous presence in multiple locations (self-multilocation), the perception of a non-terrestrial environment like heaven, and telepathy with earthly and non-earthly beings.

The OBE, in particular, is an experience in which the individual perceives themselves as separating from their physical body, while maintaining a state of full consciousness or a state that transcends normal consciousness. As described by Bünning and Blanke (2005), the OBE can be characterized by three main phenomena: (i) disembodiment, the sensation of being outside one's body; (ii) the perception of the world from an elevated and distant visuo-spatial perspective, while maintaining an egocentric point of view; and (iii) autoscopy, the impression of seeing one's physical body from this external perspective. These elements make the OBE a phenomenon that has fascinated humanity since ancient times, finding a place in myths, folklore, and spiritual experiences of many cultures.

Recent research has begun to investigate the triggers and neurological correlates of OBEs. Studies conducted by Blanke and colleagues (2005) suggest that these experiences may result from a functional disintegration in low-level multisensory processes, associated with abnormal self-processing at the level of the temporoparietal junction of the brain. This dysfunction could explain why OBEs are perceived as "real" experiences and why they have such a profound impact on individual consciousness.

It is important to note that while OBEs are often associated with NDEs, they can also occur in other circumstances, such as during sleep, drug abuse, or general anesthesia. These triggers have been widely documented in the literature, supporting the idea that OBEs may emerge from specific neurophysiological conditions, rather than exclusively spiritual or supernatural events.

In the next chapter, we will explore the personal accounts of those who have had a near-death experience (NDE). These stories, drawn from verified clinical reports, have been rigorously collected by doctors and scientists and have found their place in prestigious scientific publications. To make these narratives more accessible and engaging, they have been adapted into a narrative form, while maintaining a solid anchoring to the reported facts. The goal is to offer the reader a more intimate and personal view of these extraordinary experiences, allowing them to better understand the human and emotional dimensions of such events.

References

Alexander E. Milioni di Farfalle. Italia: Mondadori Eds; 2013.

Agrillo C. Near-death experience: out-of-body and out-of-brain. Rev Gen Psychol. 2011;15: 1–10. doi:10.1037/a0021992-

Appelby L. Near-death experience: analogous to other stress induced physiological phenomena. BMJ. 1989;298: 976–977.

Beauregard M, et al. Brain activity in near-death experiencers during a meditative state. Resuscitation 2009;80:1006–10.

Blagov PS, et al. Four dimensions of self-defining memories (specificity, meaning, content, and affect) and their relationships to self-restraint, distress, and repressive defensiveness. J Pers 2004;72:481–511.

Blanke et al. Stimulating illusory own-body perceptions. Nature. 222;419:269–270. doi:10.1038/419269a.

Bókkon I. Phosphene phenomenon: a new concept. Biosystems. 2008;92:168–174. doi:10.1016/j.biosystems.2008.02.002-

Bókkon I, et al. Brilliant lights by bioluminescent photons in near-death experiences. Med. Hypotheses. 2012;79: 47–49. doi:10.1016/j.mehy.2012.03.028.

Brooks D. The neural Buddhists. The New York Times. May 13, 2008.

Bourdin P, et al. A Virtual Outof-Body Experience Reduces Fear of Death. PLoS One 2017; 12:e0169343. doi:10.1371/journal.pone.0169343.

Bünning S, et al. The out-of-body experience: precipitating factors and neural correlates. Prog Brain Res. 2005;150:331-350. doi: 10.1016/S0079-6123(05)50024-4.

Cassol H, et al. Memories of near-death experiences: are they self-defining? Neurosci Conscious 2019 Mar 1;2019(1):niz002. doi: 10.1093/nc/niz002.

Carr DB. Endorphins at the approach of death. Lancet. 1981;1:390. doi:10.1016/S0140-6736(81)91714-1.

Chawla et al.. Surges of electroencephalogram activity at the time of death: a case series. J Palliat Med. 2009;12:1095–1100. doi:10.1089/jpm.2009.0159.

Chandler M. Self-continuity in suicidal and nonsuicidal adolescents. New Dir Child Dev 1994;55–70

Charland-Verville V, et al. Near-death experiences in non-life-threatening events and coma of different etiologies. Front Hum Neurosci 2014;8:203

Chirico F. Spiritual well-being in the 21st century: It is time to review the current WHO's health definition. J Health Soc Sci 2016;1(1):11-16.

DeAngulo JM, et al. Health paradigm shifts in the 20th century. Christian J Global Health 2015;2(1):49–58. doi: 10.15566/cjgh.v2i1.37

Engel GL. How much longer must medicine's science be bound by a seventeenth century world view? Psychother Psychosom 1992;57(1–2):3–16. doi: 10.1159/000288568.

Facco et al. Near-death experiences between science and prejudice. Front Hum Neurosci. 2012; 6:209. doi:10.3389/fnhum.2012.00209.

Fenwick et al. End of life experiences and their implications for palliative care. Int J Environ Stud. 2007;64(3):315-323. doi:10.1080/00207230701394458.

French CC. Near-death experiences in cardiac arrest survivors. Prog Brain Res 2005; 150:351-67

Greyson B. The near-death experience scale. Construction, reliability, and validity. J Nerv Ment Dis 1983;171:369–75.

Greyson B. The near-death experience as a focus of clinical attention. J Nerv Ment Dis 1997;185:327–34.

Greyson B. Near-death experiences In Cardena E, Lynn S, Krippner S (eds), Varieties of Anomalous Experiences: Examining the Scientific Evidence. Washington, DC: American Psychological Association, 2000a, 315–52

Greyson B. Dissociation in people who have near-death experiences: out of their bodies or out of their minds? Lancet 2000b;355:460–3

Greyson B. Western scientific approaches to near-death experiences. Humanities 2015;4(4):775–96. doi: 10.3390/h4040775.

Groth-Marnat G, et al. Altered beliefs, attitudes, and behaviors following near-death experiences. J Hum Psychol 1998;38:110–25. 10.1177/00221678980383005.

Habek D, et al. Near-Death Experiences in Case of Severe Obstetrics Shock. Psychiatr Danub 2022 Fall;34(3):525-526.

Halverson WH. A Concise Introduction to Philosophy. New York: Random House, 1976.

Hession A, et al. End-of-life dreams and visions: A systematic integrative review. Palliative Support Care. 2022; 1-10. doi:10.1017/S1478951522000876.

Imaizumi S, et al. Chemiluminescence in hypoxic brain–the first report. correlation between energy metabolism and free radical reaction. Stroke. 1984;15: 1061–1065. doi:10.1161/01.STR.15.6.1061-

Jansen KLR. Neuroscience and the near-death experience: roles for the NMSA-PCP receptor, the sigma receptor and the end psychosis. Med Hypotheses 1990;31:25–9

Jansen KLR. The Ketamine Model of the Near-Death Experience: A Central Role for the N-Methyl-D-Aspartate Receptor. Journal of Near-Death Studies 1997;16, 5–26. https://doi.org/10.1023/A:1025055109480.

Lempert T, et al. Syncope and near-death experience. Lancet 1994;344:829–30.

Long M, et al. Evidence of the Afterlife. Louisiana: Harper Collins Publishers, 2010.

Long J. Near-death experience. Evidence for their reality. Mo Med 2014; 111:372-80.

Long J, et al. Evidence of the Afterlife: The Science of Near-Death Experiences. HarperOne. 2010.

Martial C, et al. Fantasy proneness correlates with the intensity of near-death experiences. Front Psychiatry 2018;9:190.

Martial C, et al. The Near-Death Experience Content (NDE-C) scale: Development and psychometric validation. Conscious Cogn 2020; 86:103049. doi:10.1016/j.concog.2020.103049.

Moody RA. The Light Beyond. Bantam: Random House. 2005;224.

Murphy T. Near-death experiences in Thailand. J. Near Death Stud. 2001;19: 161–178.

Noyes R. Jr. Attitude change following near-death experiences. Psychiatry 1980;43,234–42. 10.1080/00332747.1980.11024070.

Parnia S, et al. A qualitative and quantitative study of the incidence, features, and etiology of near-death experiences in cardiac arrest survivors. Resuscitation 2001;48:149–56.

Parnia S, et al. Near death experiences, cognitive function and psychological outcomes of surviving cardiac arrest. Resuscitation 2007; 74:215-21.

Parnia S. Understanding the cognitive experience of death and the near-death experience. QJM 2017;110,67–9. 10.1093/qjmed/hcw185.

Rabitti E, et al. Hospice Patients' End-of-Life Dreams and Visions: A Systematic Review of Qualitative Studies. Am J Hosp Palliat Care. 2024;41(1):99–112. doi:10.1177/10499091231163571.

Ring K. Life at Death: A Scientific Investigation of the Near-Death Experience. Coward Mc Cann, 1980.

Ring K. Heading toward Omega: In Search of the Meaning of the Near-Death Experience. William Morrow and Company, 1984.

Ring K. Heading Toward Omega: In Search of the Meaning of the Near-Death Experience. New York: William Morrow, 1984.

Schwaninger J, et al. A prospective analysis of near-death experiences in cardiac arrest patients. J Near-Death Stud 2002;20:215–32.

Strassman R. DMT: The Spirit Molecule. Rochester: Park Street Press, 2001.

Suzuki, et al. Chemiluminescence in hypoxic brain—the second report: cerebral protective effect of mannitol, vitamin E and glucocorticoid. Stroke. 1985;16:695–700. doi:10.1161/01.STR.16.4.695.

Timmermann C, et al. DMT Models the near-death experience. Front Psychol 2018;9:1424.

Sani F. Self Continuity: Individual and Collective Perspectives. New York, NY: Psychology Press, 2008.

Van Lommel P, et al. Near-death experience in survivors of cardiac arrest: a prospective study in the Netherlands. Lancet 2001;358:2039–45.

Van Lommel P, et al. Near-death experience in survivors of cardiac arrest: a prospective study in the Netherlands. Parapsychology 2017;91–97. 10.4324/9781315247366-5.

Hashemi A, et al. Explanation of near-death experiences: a systematic analysis of case reports and qualitative research. Front Psychol 2023 Apr 20;14:1048929. doi: 10.3389/fpsyg.2023.1048929.

Khanna S, et al. Daily spiritual experiences before and after near-death experiences. Psychol Relig Spiritual 2014;6, 302. 10.1037/a0037258.

Khanna S, et al. Near-death experiences and posttraumatic growth. J Nerv Ment Dis 2015;203(10):749–755. doi: 10.1097/NMD.0000000000000362.

Knoblauch H, et al. Different kinds of near-death experience: a report on a survey of near-death experiences in Germany. J Near-Death Stud 2011;20,15–29. 10.1023/A:1011112727078.

Kopel J. Near-death experiences in medicine. Proc (Bayl Univ Med Cent) 2019 Jan 11;32(1):163-164. doi: 10.1080/08998280.2018.1542478.

Chapter 2: The Haunting Journey of Dr. Bettina Peyton

A sinister storm enveloped Boston, its torrential fury mirroring the anguish that permeated the city hospital. Raindrops pelted the windows with a frantic, ominous rhythm, creating a dark harmony in the emergency department.

Nurses, panic evident in their eyes, rushed from room to room, pushing carts laden with medications. Doctors, usually calm and composed, whispered among themselves in small clusters, their brows furrowed and their expressions alarmed.

Amidst the turmoil, Dr. Bettina Peyton, an emergency medicine specialist, performed her duties with determination. She had once led the department, and her presence commanded respect and admiration from colleagues and patients alike.

But now, she was at the center of everything that was happening: Dr. Peyton lay motionless in a room bathed in a spectral light, on the emergency medical bed. The lamp cast eerie reflections on the walls, creating a surreal and unsettling atmosphere. Scenes from the doctor's life unfolded like a film: the grueling years of medical training, the joy of giving birth to her twin sons, the many happy moments spent with her husband, Mark.

However, as the night wore on, the happy and nostalgic images of her life transformed into increasingly disturbing visions. Memories became distorted, showing threatening figures that seemed to emerge from the recesses of her mind. Bettina felt a shiver of terror run down her spine as she tried to distinguish reality from imagination, aware that something sinister was about to happen—something that would change her existence and that of those close to her forever.

Her pregnancy, a journey that should have been marked by maternal warmth and joy, had proven dangerous from the beginning for Bettina. The memories of the twins' birth were overshadowed by the harsh reality of what was happening. Every heartbeat of her little one, every kick, seemed like a possible step toward catastrophe.

Dr. Peyton's second pregnancy had been risky from the start, and every test, every checkup, had fueled growing anxiety. Every sign of life inside her was met with a mix of hope and fear.

Mark, usually a steadfast point of reference, seemed adrift. He paced restlessly back and forth outside the room, his face etched with worry, unable to find a moment of peace. Every second felt like an eternity; every whisper a harbinger of doom. The tension in the air was palpable, and the fear of losing everything they loved was unbearable.

Bettina, despite everything, tried to maintain her calm, relying on her experience and inner strength. But even she felt the shadow of doubt creeping into her heart as the storm raged both outside and within her.

Inside the dimly lit room, an overwhelming pain engulfed Bettina, obliterating the thin line between the material world and the ethereal. Reality fragmented, giving way to an otherworldly plane. This realm of light and shadow was a reflection of the very essence of existence. The air, charged with an arcane energy, pulsed with life force, and from this vast space emanated a melancholic and enchanting melody at the same time.

Shadowy, formless, and intangible figures emerged from that vastness. Their ever-changing forms danced on the precipice of the unknown until, suddenly, they morphed into the faces of Bettina's deceased grandparents. These images, untouched by the passage of time, communicated in a way that transcended words. Intense emotions, deep memories, and ancient wisdom flowed, painting a vivid picture of the lost family Bettina no longer remembered clearly.

The energy of these familial spirits seemed to want to reassure her, offering comfort in the midst of her pain. Bettina felt the warmth of a forgotten love envelop her, infusing her with a strength she didn't know she had. However, even this moment of connection was tinged with a deep sadness, a reminder of the fragility of life and the thin veil that separates the world of the living from that of the dead.

But amidst all this, a terrifying vision paralyzed Bettina. Her body lay lifeless on the hospital bed, and she saw herself from above, surrounded by colleagues and friends, noticing her husband, devastated by catastrophic thoughts of what was happening.

At the same time, an irresistible force began to pull Bettina away from the tranquil embrace of her grandparents. The surreal landscape, the beautiful yet unsettling music, began to evaporate. With a jarring impact, Bettina was once again confined within her fragile body, the pain amplified tenfold.

The consequences of this journey were seismic. The world knew Dr. Peyton as a woman and a physician of great scientific rigor, but her harrowing journey had irreparably blurred those boundaries. The sparkle in her eyes had been replaced by a depth that spoke of realms beyond human understanding. Bettina knew that her life would never be the same again, that her experiences on the edge of life and death had transformed her in ways no one could truly comprehend.

Dr. Peyton would later recount what she had seen in those brief but intense moments. Voices and whispers quickly spread throughout the hospital. While some doctors dismissed their colleague's experience as a side effect of the complication she had suffered, an ever-growing group of friends considered her a chosen one.

The hospital in that small town near Boston became the center of media and newspaper attention. Amid whispered conversations in the hallways and corridors, the story of the doctor who had seen and touched the afterlife sparked growing interest. Patients, nurses, and even skeptics were fascinated by her story, turning the hospital into a place of mystery and speculation.

Every word Bettina spoke was analyzed, every detail discussed and reinterpreted. Her experience was not just a medical event but a phenomenon that had opened a window into a world beyond life, a mystery that no one could ignore. And so, Dr. Peyton, once known only for her scientific rigor, became a symbol of an unfathomable mystery, a bridge between the known and the unknown.

But the repercussions of her journey were also deeply personal. From that day on, Dr. Peyton's nightmares became habitual companions of her sleep, and the unsettling melody she had heard that day was an omnipresent echo. Skeptics dismissed her experience as merely "hallucinatory," while those who believed in the afterlife looked at her with curiosity or admiration.

To find relief and understanding, Bettina began to describe her experiences in a diary. The pages filled with tormented visions and deep reflections, in an attempt to make sense of what she had experienced.

Regardless of individual beliefs, there was unanimous recognition of an undeniable truth: Dr. Peyton's journey had torn the veil, revealing the existence of something unknown and unknowable that happens at the moment of death. Her story was not just a personal account but a challenge to human understanding, an invitation to explore the boundaries between life and death, between the tangible and the transcendent.

Bettina knew her path would not be easy. Each day brought new challenges, both in reconciling her experience with everyday reality and in dealing with the various reactions of the people around her. But with every word written, with every nightmare faced, Bettina sought to find balance, a new understanding of herself and the world around her. And so, her journey continued, weaving the past with the present, mystery with science, in an unrelenting quest for truth and meaning.

As the storm outside the hospital subsided, it became evident that Dr. Peyton's journey of discovery was far from over.

Author's Note:

This story is loosely inspired by a real-life event, as documented in a case study published in the scientific article titled "Verified Account of Near-Death Experience in a Physician Who Survived Cardiac

Arrest." The article, written by Dr. Woollacott and Dr. Peyton, was published in the journal *Explore* (May-June 2021; 17(3):213-219. doi: 10.1016/j.explore.2020.03.005).

The Perspective of the On-Call Doctor

Dr. Peyton's account is not just a recounting of the clinical events experienced in the emergency room during cardiac arrest; it is also a profound reflection on the challenges and surprises that sometimes confront those who practice medicine.

As the privileged witness of an event that has challenged and continues to challenge every scientific understanding, the attending physician who was with Dr. Peyton during that unforgettable night shared his own experiences and the emotional turmoil triggered by those moments.

"When I first heard about Dr. Peyton's experience, I thought of it simply as hospital gossip. As the physician who admitted her that night in the emergency room, I was on the front line, directly witnessing the collapse of her vital signs and coordinating the efforts to stabilize her.

It's true, there were moments when we thought we might lose her. But what happened on the edge of her consciousness, and what was told to me later, I couldn't have imagined.

I've seen many patients undergo cardiac arrests or trauma, and I'm well aware of the brain's reactions. Hallucinations, lucid dreams, and even out-of-body experiences are common during such situations. However, there was something undeniably different about Dr. Peyton's case. When she finally regained consciousness, I carefully observed her eyes. They were not the eyes of someone who had just faced a life-threatening event; they were the eyes of someone who had journeyed and seen something astonishing.

While I tried to examine what had happened with the necessary clinical detachment, considering possible scientific explanations that could justify her experience, the emotional involvement and conviction with which Bettina recounted her journey were profoundly unsettling for me. However, as a firm believer in empirical evidence and the scientific method, I attempted to question what I had heard, while also trying to confront the limits of my understanding. Could there really be realms beyond our comprehension? Were the images Bettina had seen just products of some area of the brain? Were they generated by consciousness in an altered or different state from the one we inhabit when we are awake and interact with others?

In the days that followed, as her story drew the attention of everyone, whether skeptic or believer in the afterlife, I often found myself reflecting on the nature of existence, consciousness, and the mysteries of life and death. Even now, as I frequently revisit and discuss with other doctors what happened to Dr. Peyton, I must admit that this adventure has instilled in me a new sense of humility and wonder at the vastness of what remains unknown and beyond our knowledge."

In this account, we have explored the intimate and extraordinary testimony of the doctor who attended Dr. Peyton during that night. This is not just a recounting of the clinical events experienced in the emergency room but a deep reflection on the challenges and surprises that sometimes intersect the path of those who practice medicine and care for the sick. The healthcare provider can become the privileged witness of an event that challenges their understanding of the world and science.

According to the abstract of the cited article, Bettina Peyton had a Near-Death Experience (NDE) during the birth of her third child at the age of 32. The data collected by the doctors and presented in the article provide some evidence for a better understanding of such phenomena: 1) during NDEs, individuals may experience sensory perceptions that are not possible according to the materialist theory, in which consciousness is solely the result of neuronal activity in our brain; 2) NDEs lead to a fundamental change in the understanding of the nature of consciousness and the sanctity of life for those who experience them.

What Are Near-Death Experiences? The Perspective of Scientists

In 1975, the term "Near-Death Experience (NDE)" made its debut in the English vocabulary thanks to Dr. Raymond Moody, who had collected over 150 accounts from individuals who had emerged from comas (Moody, 1975). Moody coined specific and original terminology to describe NDEs, such as "out-of-body experience," "encounter with beings of light," and "life review," which have become standard terms in the study of NDEs.

The book had a huge impact not only within the scientific community but also in popular culture, inspiring films, TV series, and further academic research. Moody, being both a doctor and a philosopher, approached the study of NDEs from a unique perspective, intertwining scientific methodologies with philosophical considerations, opening new avenues of inquiry into the concept of consciousness and the survival of the individual and their personality after death.

However, descriptions and accounts of the phenomenon date back much earlier, particularly to Hieronymus Bosch's 1505 masterpiece, "The Ascent of the Blessed." Hieronymus Bosch was known for his enigmatic and symbol-rich paintings. "The Ascent of the Blessed," part of a triptych called "The Haywain," is a fascinating work depicting the souls of the righteous ascending to heaven. The work is full of mysterious symbols and open-ended interpretations. The figures represented in the painting are often interpreted as souls leaving the earthly world for an otherworldly existence, which can be seen as an ancient parallel to the modern theories on NDEs described by Moody.

While there is no universally accepted definition of NDEs, it is widely recognized that NDEs involve a series of specific cognitive events—referred to as "attributes"—that combine deeply personal, emotional, and transcendental elements (Charland-Verville, 2017). The main attributes involve sensations of levitation outside of one's physical form, experiences of intense calm, passage through a threshold (perhaps a tunnel), and movement toward an intense light (Charland-Verville, 2017; Martial et al., 2017).

NDE episodes occur in various circumstances, generally when people are facing death or perceive its imminent threat (Charland-Verville, 2014). In the following years, the study of NDEs expanded, mainly thanks to technological and scientific advancements in resuscitation methods. Consequently, these exceptional states of consciousness have been reported more frequently, with prevalence rates in scientific research ranging from 10% to 23% following resuscitation from cardiac arrest (van Lommel et al., 2001; Schwaninger et al., 2002; Greyson, 2003), but only 3% of cases after significant brain trauma, according to Hou and collaborators (2013).

Similar episodes to NDEs can also occur in different situations, such as during reflective practices (Beauregard et al., 2009) or during sudden losses of consciousness (Lempert et al., 2004). These events are labeled as NDE-like experiences ("NDEs-like"; see Charland-Verville, 2014).

Currently, distinguishing between classic NDEs (which occur in life-threatening or near-death situations) and NDE-like experiences ("NDEs-like") based solely on the descriptions of the experiencers is quite challenging, as both categories exhibit overlapping patterns and meet Greyson's "NDE criteria."

Greyson's criteria consist of 16 indicators and a minimum score of 7 out of 32 for an experience to be recognized as a valid NDE (Charland-Verville, 2014; Greyson, 1983). Greyson's criteria are a standardized tool used by researchers and scientists to assess both the presence and the depth of a near-death experience. Bruce Greyson developed this scale in 1983 to quantify NDEs and study them systematically.

The Greyson Scale includes 16 indicators, grouped into four main categories: cognitive, affective, paranormal, and transcendental. A score of 7 out of 32 or higher is generally considered indicative of a true NDE. Here is an overview of these indicators:

Cognitive Indicators:
- Altered perception of time.
- Accelerated thought processes.
- Vivid thoughts.
- Memory of past life events.

Affective Indicators:
- Feelings of peace or pleasantness.
- Feelings of joy.
- Feelings of universal love.
- Encounter with spiritual beings or deceased individuals.

Paranormal Indicators:
- Out-of-body experiences (seeing one's body from an external perspective).
- Visions of remote places or events (remote viewing).
- Hearing unusual sounds or voices.

Transcendental Indicators:
- Experience of a symbolic boundary or barrier.
- Arrival in another world or non-terrestrial dimension.
- Encounter with a presence or being of light.
- A profound cosmic understanding or "enlightenment."

These indicators are used to determine not only the presence of an NDE but also its intensity. The Greyson Scale is widely recognized and used in numerous scientific and clinical studies on near-death experiences and continues to be a fundamental reference in the field of NDE research.

It is significant to note that not all NDEs are described as uplifting or enhancing the previous state; about 14% of such experiences are distressing or deeply unsettling (Cassol et al., 2019). In other words, while many NDEs are described in terms of a profound sense of "peace" and "transcendental enlightenment," a notable percentage of them induce fear, isolation, or despair. This aspect of NDEs underscores the diversity and complexity of the phenomenon, highlighting the need for a mature approach in supporting and treating patients who have experienced an NDE, regardless of the nature of their experiences.

In the future, it is essential that research continues to explore these experiences from multiple perspectives—neurological, psychological, cultural, and spiritual—to better decipher what happens when the boundary between life and death seems to be crossed. Only through interdisciplinary dialogue and careful attention to the patients' narratives can we hope to come closer to a more complete understanding of NDEs and their impact on the individual and society.

References

Beauregard, M. et al. (2009) Brain activity in near-death experiencers during a meditative state. Resuscitation 80, 1006–1010

Cassol, H. et al. (2019) A systematic analysis of distressing near-death experience accounts. Memory 27, 1122–1129.

Charland-Verville, V. et al. (2014) Near-death experiences in non-life-threatening events and coma of different etiologies. Front. Hum. Neurosci. 8, 203

Charland-Verville, V. et al. (2017) Near-death experiences: actual considerations. In Coma and Disorders of Consciousness (3rd ed) (Schnakers, C. and Laureys, S., eds), pp. 235–263, Springer

Greyson, B. (1983) The near-death experience scale. Construction, reliability, and validity. J. Nerv. Ment. Dis. 171, 369–375

Greyson, B. (2003) Incidence and correlates of near-death experiences in a cardiac care unit. Gen. Hosp. Psychiatry 25, 269–276

Hou, Y. et al. (2013) Infrequent near-death experiences in severe brain injury survivors - a quantitative and qualitative study. Ann. Indian Acad. Neurol. 16, 75–81

Lempert, T. et al. (1994) Syncope and near-death experience. Lancet 344, 829–830

9. Martial, C. et al. (2017) Temporality of features in near-death experience narratives. Front. Hum. Neurosci. 11, 311

Moody, R.A., ed (1975) *Life after Life*, Bantam Books

Schwaninger, J. et al. (2002) A prospective analysis of near-death experiences in cardiac arrest patients. J. Near-Death Stud. 20, 215–232

van Lommel, P. et al. (2001) Near-death experience in cardiac arrest survivors: a prospective study in the Netherlands. Lancet 358, 2039–2045

Chapter 3: A Doctor's Journey

"In the sweltering summer of 1977, an incident involving a respiratory crisis profoundly changed my personal and professional life, dispelling any residual fear of death. From that moment on, a fleeting glimpse of the majesty of the Divine has accompanied me, the result of a near-death experience (NDE).

At the time, I was a 22-year-old medical student. Immediately after taking an exam, my vision began to blur, worsening rapidly and steadily. I also felt a pronounced heaviness in my eyelids. After finishing the exam, I immediately called my father, an experienced physician, and met him at the local emergency room, where I was examined by a team of specialists. My health quickly deteriorated into descending paralysis.

The neurologist suspected it might be Guillain-Barré syndrome, likely the Jacksonian variant, triggered by the Zika virus. Just before I was transported to the Pulmonology department for lung function tests, a doctor decided to administer a test with physostigmine.

Unfortunately, he administered an excessive dose. My condition took a dangerous turn, culminating in acute respiratory collapse. As I lay in the respiratory medicine room, the strength to breathe left me, and darkness fell.

Suddenly, my awareness elevated, transforming me into an external observer, suspended about 30 feet above my body lying on the ground. The scene unfolded like a film reel, allowing me to perceive every detail through barriers, with a complete 360-degree panoramic view.

I could see the doctors and nurses frantically working around my body, their expressions of concern and urgency clearly visible. I heard fragments of their conversations, words filled with tension and alarm. In that moment of detachment, fear and pain seemed distant, replaced by a sense of peace and clarity.

As I watched the scene, I was enveloped by a warm, embracing light that emanated a feeling of unconditional love and serenity. In that light, I saw familiar figures, some of whom I had lost long ago. They smiled at me, radiating a reassuring calm.

There were no words, only a deep, silent communication that conveyed the certainty that everything would be alright, regardless of the outcome. I was in a place of pure essence, where time seemed suspended, and life and death merged into a single continuum.

Despite hearing the voices and frantic movement around me, I felt strangely detached. Looking down at that inert body, I felt neither worry nor fear; instead, it seemed almost meaningless. My perception of myself and the world around me was completely transformed: what was once vital now appeared as a mere empty shell.

In contrast, a radiant, pulsating light drew me from my right. It radiated a warmth, love, and welcome that were indescribable. Attracted by its warm embrace, I rose toward that light, leaving behind the earthly darkness. About halfway through, I realized I had passed into another life. Yet the pull I felt toward the luminous entity was irresistible, and a deep sense of unity with it enveloped me as I immersed myself in its glowing embrace.

Around me, souls shimmered with ethereal light, each radiating pure love—each was a manifestation of Divine splendor. Their identities remained a mystery, but their love was undeniable. There, my soul felt completely fulfilled. That place was evidently devoid of earthly imperfections, radiating only pure love and light. It was a sacred place that felt intimately familiar, as if I had once come from there. In that celestial realm, my understanding expanded enormously. Communication was fluid; there was no need for words; intention was enough.

The souls around me were filled with light and shared deep knowledge. They explained that Earth is a school of experience, rich in lessons and challenges, all aimed at honoring the Divine and helping our fellow beings. On Earth, we struggle with our virtues and flaws. In contrast, what exists in the divine realm is pure, uncontaminated by earthly afflictions, free from disputes or struggles, only an endless reservoir of love, understanding, and enlightenment.

The souls conveyed messages of hope, love, and guidance. They emphasized that while Earth is transient and full of trials, it offers invaluable lessons for the soul's growth and evolution. Every challenge, every pain, every joy is a steppingstone on the path of spiritual growth, a test of our resilience, compassion, and integrity. Every act of kindness, every gesture of love, is a beacon of light that pierces the intrinsic darkness of the world.

As I was enraptured by the ethereal beauty and profound revelations, a distant but familiar sensation began to pull me back. Whispered voices, faint but growing clearer, called me back. As inviting and comforting as it was, the luminous realm began to fade, replaced by a more corporeal reality.

With a sudden jolt, I found myself in the hospital's Pulmonology Unit. My senses were immediately flooded with the smell of antiseptic, the distant hum of machines, and the palpable relief in the room. The medical staff, including my father, surrounded me, their faces marked by surprise and relief. I had been resuscitated.

The following days were a whirlwind of medical tests, discussions, and treatments. As I regained my strength, the memories of the NDE I had experienced remained vivid. The dichotomy between having experienced the serene beauty of the otherworldly realm and the chaotic urgency of the hospital was overwhelming.

I shared my experience with a few close individuals, including my father. While some met my account with skepticism, many listened with rapt attention, absorbing the profound messages and implications of what I had lived through. It became clear that this experience was not just for my benefit, but was meant to be shared to offer hope and comfort to others.

Years later, as a practicing physician, I often recalled what had happened to me that day. The memory of that experience transformed my approach to medicine, driving me to treat not just the illness but the whole person. My patients often commented on my empathetic approach; when possible, I shared with them fragments of my journey.

The NDE became a pivotal event in my life, a constant reminder of the transient nature of our earthly existence and the eternal nature of the soul. That experience taught me the importance of love, compassion, and understanding. More important than anything else, it confirmed to me that death is not an end, but a passage to a realm of limitless love and light.

In the years that followed, I devoted myself more to researching near-death experiences. I attended conferences, participated in discussions, and collaborated on research papers. The medical community was divided: while some doctors were eager to understand and validate these experiences, others dismissed them as neurological anomalies. But for me and many others who had lived through them, the NDE was as real as the air we breathe.

My practice thrived, not only because of my medical expertise but because patients felt heard and understood. Word spread and I became known as the doctor who believed in the "afterlife." Surprisingly, this title attracted more patients than it discouraged. People were curious, eager for knowledge about what existed beyond the boundaries of our mortal realm. And while I couldn't provide all the answers, I could offer a perspective that few others could."

This story is loosely inspired by a real event, as recounted in a clinical case study published in the scientific article written by Dr. JR Hausheer, titled "A Physician's Near-Death Experience," and published in the journal *Narrative Inquiry in Bioethics* (2020;10(1):11-14. doi: 10.1353/nib.2020.0001).

The narrative is based on real events described in the article, but it also includes fictional elements to enrich the storytelling and deepen the thematic reflections. Therefore, while some details and situations are drawn from documented experiences, other aspects have been adapted or invented for narrative purposes.

Personal Reflections

When I began recounting near-death experiences, my primary goal was to clarify how science, spirituality, and human resilience intertwine in complex and profound ways.

The story of the medical student is not only a testimony to the ethereal realms that some believe exist beyond our earthly existence but also underscores the fragility and beauty of life.

The detailed description of the out-of-body experience felt by the young doctor in his student days, the vivid images, and the deep emotional connections experienced during the event push us to question the boundaries of our knowledge, our understanding of consciousness, and the very nature of reality.

This juxtaposition between science and spirituality underscores the central theme of this book: the vastness of the unknown that remains to be explored, understood, and accepted. Like all the other stories I've chosen to tell, this narrative serves as a reminder that perhaps death is not an end but a transformation, not a void, but a different kind of existence. Whether or not one believes in the metaphysical aspects of such experiences, it is undeniable that they leave an indelible mark on those who live through them, changing their view of life, death, and everything in between.

In my journey as a researcher, I have learned that stories like these have the power to bring comfort, stimulate introspection, and challenge our beliefs and biases. I sincerely hope that readers approach this case, and others like it, with an open mind and heart, as between the lines of what you will read lies a universal truth about humanity's eternal quest for understanding and connection with the divine.

What makes the case just described particularly fascinating is the young age of the individual involved. As a medical student, the young man was at the beginning of his career, ready to immerse himself in the world of science and medicine, but still unconditioned by the knowledge and experiences he had not yet fully acquired. His journey, in a sudden situation that had seriously threatened his life, tested everything he knew and believed he knew.

Having collected and studied several near-death experiences, I have understood that every story is unique, but there are often common threads: a sense of peace, an encounter with radiant light, communication without words, and a deep sense of interconnectedness.

The narrative also highlights the challenge of integrating such profound personal experiences into one's professional life, especially in a field guided by scientific evidence like medicine. The potential skepticism of colleagues, the struggle to articulate the inarticulable, and the quest for balance between science and spirituality are challenges that many people with similar experiences face.

Stories like these, challenge our boundaries of understanding. They invite us to dig deeper, to question, to seek, and ultimately to embrace the mysteries of life. It is remarkable to note how these experiences have involved not only patients but also doctors themselves, who then chose to recount them through scientific publications.

To return to the book I mentioned in the Introduction, written by neuroscientist Dr. Eben Alexander, author of *Proof of Heaven*, the fact that there are doctors who rationally leave personal testimonies, who decide to share with the academic world and the general public is significant. It is extraordinary that professionals accustomed to working with scientific rigor find the courage and the will to explore and share these experiences, opening new doors to human understanding. These accounts not only enrich the debate between science and spirituality but invite us to explore with open minds and hearts, always ready to be amazed by the unknown.

What Is an Out-of-Body Experience to Medical Science?

An out-of-body experience (OBE) refers to the sensation where one perceives that their consciousness (or awareness) temporarily detaches from the physical body, allowing them to observe the surrounding environment from an external point of view. This sensation is often described as floating or being suspended above, in an elevated position relative to one's body.

This phenomenon is commonly associated with near-death experiences (NDEs). Many who have had an NDE have survived acute and severe medical events, such as cardiac arrest (Long, 2014).

Scientific research has investigated the accuracy of observations made during OBEs. In a pioneering study by Dr. Michael Sabom, patients who had experienced cardiac arrests and had an NDE, including OBEs, were able to provide more accurate descriptions of their resuscitations compared to a control group of patients who had cardiac events without an NDE (Sabom, 1982).

Dr. Penny Sartori conducted a study following Dr. Sabom's methodology, arriving at a similar conclusion: those who had experienced an NDE could often recall and describe details of their resuscitation with incredible precision, while the control group's accounts were generally less accurate (Sartori, 2008).

Two large retrospective studies have further confirmed the accuracy of OBE observations. One, conducted by Dr. Janice Holden, examined published academic content and identified 89 clinical case reports of NDEs with OBEs (Holden, 2009), revealing that an astonishing 92% of them could be considered accurate.

Another study analyzed 617 NDEs shared on the "NDERF" website, and of the 287 NDEs with detailed descriptions of OBEs, a full 97.6% were entirely realistic. Notably, 23% of these individuals had undertaken personal investigations after the incidents that led to their near-death state, and none found discrepancies in the descriptions of their out-of-body experiences (Long et al., 2010).

The high consistency in the accuracy of OBE observations during NDEs challenges our current understanding of brain function. Some OBEs report observations made while the individual was clinically comatose or describe events far from their physical body, outside sensory awareness (van Lommel et al., 2001).

There are also cases where the events observed were completely unexpected, contradicting the idea that these experiences are simply illusory memories or inventions based on preconceived expectations about near-death events. Albert Einstein's quote, "A person should seek what is, and not what they think should be," aptly underscores the importance of conducting an objective investigation to understand such phenomena.

These experiences, which remain enigmatic, urge us to look beyond our current understanding and remain open to the possibility of new scientific discoveries (Long, 2014). The accuracy of perceptions reported by individuals in OBE states during NDEs invites serious reflection on how science should approach phenomena that traditionally lie at the fringes of its investigative field.

These experiences suggest that there may be an aspect of human reality not yet fully understood, one that transcends the limits of the physical body and opens up to a dimension that has been little explored until now. As we continue to explore and study OBEs and NDEs, it is essential to maintain an open and inclusive approach, embracing both rigorous scientific methodologies and a sincere respect for individuals' personal experiences.

Only through such a balance can we hope to approach a more complete understanding of these mysterious and fascinating phenomena. In conclusion, the investigation of out-of-body experiences not only enriches our scientific knowledge but invites us to reflect on the nature of human existence.

Perhaps, as suggested by these experiences, death is not the end of everything, but a passage to a different state. If so, new perspectives would open up on the continuity of consciousness beyond physical boundaries. As we continue our journey through the vast and intricate landscape of human knowledge, these stories remind us that much remains to be discovered and that every answer brings with it new questions, equally profound and stimulating.

References

Holden JM. *Veridical perception in near-death experiences.* In: Holden JM, Greyson B, James D, editors. *The Handbook of Near-Death Experiences: Thirty Years of Investigation.* Santa Barbara, CA: Praeger/ABC-CLIO; 2009. pp. 185–211

Long J. *Near-death experience. Evidence for their reality.* Mo Med. 2014 Sep-Oct;111(5):372-80.

Long J, et al. *Evidence of the Afterlife: The Science of Near-Death Experiences.* New York, NY: HarperCollins; 2010. pp. 74–78.

Sabom M. *Recollections of Death: A Medical Investigation.* New York: Simon & Schuster; 1982.

Sartori P. *The Near-Death Experiences of Hospitalized Intensive Care Patients: A Five-Year Clinical Study.* Lewiston, NY: Edwin Mellen Press; 2008

van Lommel P, et al. *Near-death experience in cardiac arrest survivors: A prospective study in the Netherlands.* Lancet. 2001; 358:2039–2045.

Chapter 4: Three Journeys Beyond the Border Between Science and Spirituality

In my clinical research on intriguing cases of near-death experiences (NDEs), I came across a scientific article published in a journal indexed in PubMed/Medline, which presented three authentic accounts of NDEs. The cases I am about to share involve NDEs that occurred following severe head trauma, critical illnesses, comas, and suicide attempts. Particularly fascinating is the fact that all these patients described an out-of-body experience (OBE).

Initially, the patients could vividly recall the events during their NDE, but as time passed, their memories became less clear. The scientific article also examines potential cultural and sociodemographic factors that might have influenced the accounts of these near-death experiences. Theories about the reasons behind such experiences have been explored by scientists with extensive references to existing scientific literature.

Ultimately, however, the article poses a provocative question: Are these experiences mere hallucinations, or could they offer a glimpse into the afterlife? While opinions remain divided, one thing is certain: as more data and similar cases emerge in the future, the debate will only intensify.

The First Case Study

A 30-year-old woman, a college graduate, Hindu by religion, and married with a 5-month-old child, was rushed to the hospital with a severe head injury and a Glasgow Coma Scale score of E1 V1 M2. She underwent surgery for an acute subdural hematoma on the left side and was placed on a ventilator for 8 days, remaining unconscious for about two months. After this period, she began a slow recovery that lasted a year.

During her period of unconsciousness, the patient described being immersed in a bright light in which she was floating. She recounted going to a place she described as "heaven," where she encountered a pantheon of gods organized in a hierarchy. She described the presence of the trinity of Brahma, Vishnu, and Shiva but stated that they were hierarchically inferior to "Om," a supreme luminous being.

Surprisingly, during her out-of-body experience, she could recall technical conversations between the doctors regarding the ventilator, the endotracheal tube, and the tracheotomy. Despite her reluctance, she reported being "sent back" by "Om."

Over the next seven years, the patient gradually forgot many details of her experience, but her conviction about the reality of what she had experienced remained unchanged.

The Second Case Study

A 45-year-old woman, a devout Catholic, was admitted to the hospital following a severe car accident. She sustained multiple traumas, including a skull fracture and internal bleeding. She was immediately taken for emergency surgery and placed in a medically induced coma to manage brain swelling. She remained in this state for three weeks.

During the coma, the patient described an extraordinary experience. She found herself in a vast field of light, surrounded by angelic figures radiating love and serenity. She reported perceiving a divine presence, identified as Jesus, who communicated with her telepathically, telling her not to fear and to trust. The angelic figures showed her moments from her life, helping her to understand the spiritual lessons behind each event.

Astonishingly, the patient was able to recall conversations between the medical staff during her coma, including specific details about the surgical procedures and discussions about her critical condition. Despite her initially severe condition, she began a slow but steady recovery, which required several months of rehabilitation.

Seven years later, the patient had forgotten many details of her experience, but her belief in the reality of the event remained strong. She reported that the experience profoundly changed her life, strengthening her faith and giving her a new perspective on life and death.

The Third Case Study

A 4-year-old boy, Hindu by religion, was brought to the emergency room in a state of hypotensive shock due to gastroenteritis with dehydration. The child had no pulse and was unconscious. Over the course of about a week, his condition gradually improved. After extubation, he began to describe his experience of being "among silver-white clouds" with a sensation of "time dilation," stating that he felt like he had been there for months, even though his altered state of consciousness lasted only a week.

Eventually, the boy forgot most of the experience he had. The family's reaction was initially neutral, and they advised the boy not to dwell on what had happened.

Personal Reflections

These three stories are freely based on and inspired by the three clinical cases reported in the scientific publication by Purkayastha M and Mukherjee KK, titled *Three cases of near death experience: Is it physiology, physics or philosophy?* published in *Annals of Neurosciences* (July 2012; 19(3):104-6. doi: 10.5214/ans.0972.7531.190303).

These cases, which explore near-death experiences (NDEs) in different clinical contexts, have prompted me to deeply reflect on the limits of our scientific understanding of consciousness and life beyond life.

In the first case, a young Hindu woman described a mystical experience during a long period of unconsciousness, in which she encountered a divine pantheon organized in a hierarchy culminating in a supreme figure called "Om." This account struck me for its complexity and the clarity with which the patient recalled technical details of medical conversations that occurred while she was in a coma. These elements challenge conventional neurophysiological explanations and suggest the existence of dimensions of consciousness that may extend beyond the physical body.

The second clinical case tells the story of a Catholic woman who, during an induced coma, experienced an encounter with angelic figures and the presence of Jesus. Her descriptions of love and serenity, along with her ability to recall medical conversations that occurred while she was unconscious, led me to ponder the possibility that these experiences are not simply stress-induced hallucinations but rather visions of a deeper, universal spiritual reality.

Finally, the third case involves a four-year-old boy who, after being resuscitated from a state of hypotensive shock, described a stay among silver-white clouds and a dilation of time. The purity and simplicity of his account made me reflect on how the minds of children, not yet influenced by social constructs, may be more open to perceptions that elude adult comprehension. His sense of having spent months in a place of peace, despite the brief period of unconsciousness, raises profound questions about the nature of time and reality.

These episodes highlight how, in extreme stress situations such as cardiac arrest or shock, the brain can generate intensely real and often transcendental perceptions and sensations. However, these experiences continue to challenge traditional scientific explanations and invite us to explore with an open mind the possibilities that there are dimensions of consciousness still unknown to us.

Each case represents not just a clinical experience but an invitation to look beyond the boundaries of science, embracing the possibility that there are aspects of consciousness and existence that we cannot yet fully explain with our current tools and knowledge. These stories remind us that, in the end, the answers to the great mysteries of life may not be found in science books, but in the lived experiences of those who have touched the boundary between the world we know and what might lie beyond.

Chapter 5: A Journey Through the Tunnel: Marianne's Story

"Unpredictably and surprisingly, I passed through the tunnel quickly. However, 'quickly' might not be the most accurate term, as it wasn't really a movement. It was more like fading away only to suddenly reemerge. It was similar to a swift flash. In the end, I felt split in two. My physical body lay on the bed, and from an elevated position, I observed myself. My double, suspended from the ceiling, was watching a scene of profound clarity and truth."

This is Marianne's story, who suddenly found herself being drawn into the unknown. The world around her changed rapidly; the familiar surroundings of her bedroom vanished, replaced by a tunnel that seemed infinite. As she passed through the tunnel, she felt herself dissolve into nothingness, only to be reconstituted shortly thereafter.

Before all this happened, some images flashed rapidly before Marianne's eyes: memories of the past, forgotten dreams, and fragments of possible futures. It was a symphony of experiences, lived or yet to be lived. In one particular vision, Marianne saw herself as a child, playing with her grandmother in a sunlit garden. The air was filled with the sweet scent of blooming roses and joyful laughter, a moment of pure happiness.

As the images continued to flash before her like a movie, Marianne felt a flood of emotions within her: the loss of her grandmother, the moments of happiness not fully lived, the pain of losing her son two years earlier. Suddenly, the visions ceased, and Marianne woke up with a start. The morning sun filtered through the window, casting a warm light on her face. The memories of her journey were still fresh, and she felt a burning desire to live life to the fullest.

The Near-Death Experience as an "Alteration of the Sense of Self"

Marianne's story vividly illustrates the phenomenon of near-death experiences (NDEs), which in scientific literature are often described as alterations of the sense of self. These experiences can be likened to altered states of consciousness that occur during meditation, sleep, or under the influence of hallucinogenic substances (Baumeister et al., 2002; Dor-Ziderman et al., 2013; Nour et al., 2016). According to Martial and colleagues (2020), NDEs are moments of "altered consciousness" where individuals experience typical cognitive events, laden with emotional and spiritual nuances. Such experiences commonly arise in critical circumstances such as cardiac failure, severe injuries, brain hemorrhages, drowning, or asphyxiation (Peinkhofer et al., 2019).

NDEs can manifest during moments of perceived or real danger to one's life, such as intense anxiety, and, as mentioned, even during entirely physiological states like sleep. Cases that occur during sleep, under the influence of psychotropic substances, or during meditation are defined as "NDE-like," as they reflect the same characteristics of a "standard" NDE without an immediate threat to the person's life (Charland-Verville et al., 2014).

In scientific research, identifying participants who have had near-death or similar experiences focuses on how intensely they experienced these events. Specifically, researchers evaluate the extent to which specific characteristics emerge and with what intensity during such experiences. This approach allows for distinguishing between those who truly had an NDE and those who experienced something very similar.

The Near-Death Experience Content Scale (NDE-C) is a scientific tool introduced by researchers, validated from a psychometric standpoint, to identify the presence of NDE traits and support the academic study of this phenomenon (Martial et al., 2020; 2021).

These discoveries and psychometric tools represent an important contribution to understanding NDEs, which are complex and difficult to study phenomena. Both standard and "NDE-like" experiences continue to represent a fascinating field of study, shedding light on deep aspects of human consciousness. By studying NDEs, we not only deepen our understanding of the mind and consciousness but also explore the frontiers of our comprehension of life and death, with implications that extend well beyond the realm of science.

Returning to Marianne's story, her experience offers us a lens through which we can observe and reflect on the complexity of NDEs. Her vision of silver-white clouds, the fleeting images of her past, and the feeling of transcendent peace push us to consider the possibilities that lie beyond the boundaries of our daily reality.

Marianne brought back with her a message of hope and renewed zest for life, an invaluable gift she shared with those around her. Her story, like those of many others who have had similar experiences, reminds us that the answers we seek may not always be found in books or scientific journals but in human experiences that touch the depths of our consciousness.

In this chapter, we explored not only the personal accounts of those who have experienced an NDE but also the scientific theories that attempt to explain these phenomena. Marianne's story invites us to keep an open mind, to continue seeking answers, and to recognize that sometimes the deepest questions about life and death may not have a definitive answer. However, it is in this relentless search that the true essence of our humanity lies.

References

Baumeister RF, et al. Mystical self-loss: A challenge for psychological theory. Int. J. Psychol Relig. 2002;12:15–20. doi: 10.1207/S15327582IJPR1201_02.

Charland-Verville V, et al. Near-death experiences in non-life-threatening events and coma of different etiologies. Front Hum Neurosci. 2014;8:203. doi: 10.3389/fnhum.2014.00203.

Dor-Ziderman Y, et al. Mindfulness-induced selflessness: A MEG neurophenomenological study. Front Hum Neurosci. 2013;7:582. doi: 10.3389/fnhum.2013.00582.

Martial C, et al. Near-death experience as a probe to explore (disconnected) consciousness. TiCS. 2020;24:173–183. doi: 10.1016/j.tics.2019.12.010.

Martial C, et al. The Near-Death Experience Content (NDE-C): Development and psychometric validation. Conscious Cogn. 2020;86:103049. doi: 10.1016/j.concog.2020.103049.

Martial C, et al. Losing the Self in Near-Death Experiences: The Experience of Ego-Dissolution Brain Sci. 2021 Jul 14;11(7):929. doi: 10.3390/brainsci11070929.

Nour MM, et al. Ego-Dissolution and Psychedelics: Validation of the Ego-Dissolution Inventory (EDI) Front Hum Neurosci. 2016;10:269. doi: 10.3389/fnhum.2016.00269.

Peinkhofer C, et al. Semiology and mechanisms of near-death experiences. Curr Neurol Neurosci Rep. 2019;19:9. doi: 10.1007/s11910-019-0983-2.

Chapter 6: Near-Death Experiences in ICU Survivors: Findings from a Follow-Up Study

Near-death experiences (NDEs) are fascinating phenomena that often occur in extreme crisis situations, such as during cardiac arrest or severe trauma. In this chapter, we will explore a recent scientific study that investigated NDEs in patients who survived intensive care (ICU) stays.

It is not uncommon for ICU patients to report unusual experiences, ranging from a sense of harmony with their surroundings to more complex phenomena like full-fledged near-death experiences. A recent study by Rousseau and colleagues (2023) delved into the characteristics and possible long-term impact of NDE memories reported by ICU survivors.

The follow-up study presented in this chapter, conducted by Martial and colleagues (2024), collected and analyzed the results of several follow-up interviews (at 1 month and 1 year after ICU discharge) with a group of ICU survivors previously enrolled in Rousseau's study. The aim was to characterize their memories of the ICU stay and any NDEs they experienced, as well as the potential consequences these NDEs had on their lifestyle, well-being, worldview, and personal beliefs.

Study Methods

The prospective study by Martial and colleagues enrolled 126 adult survivors of prolonged ICU stays (more than seven days). Among them, 19 (15%) reported having had a near-death experience, identified using the Greyson NDE Scale. These patients underwent a semi-structured interview one month after discharge to assess the characteristics of their memory and the life-threatening situation associated with their NDE. One year after inclusion, all patients, regardless of whether they remembered an NDE, were contacted for a follow-up evaluation using the Greyson NDE Scale and were questioned about their ICU experience and their views on death.

Study Results

The Greyson NDE Scale revealed that the most frequently reported characteristics among ICU survivors were altered time perception, heightened senses, a "life review," and encounters with a mystical presence. Notably, NDE memories remained vivid over time, retaining a high number of phenomenological features, such as detailed visual recollections and the emotions experienced. A year after their ICU stay, a small percentage of patients in both the NDE and non-NDE groups reported feeling less afraid of death.

Life Review in Near-Death Experiences

The life review during a near-death experience (NDE) is a complex phenomenon involving the detailed recollection of significant events from one's life. This experience offers a unique opportunity for reflection and learning, often leading to lasting personal transformations. Here are some key features of this phenomenon:

- **Detailed Recollection:** Individuals who undergo a life review during an NDE report seeing or reliving past events with extraordinary clarity and detail. These memories can include childhood moments, significant relationships, important decisions, and other key life events.
- **Holistic Perspective:** During the life review, individuals may perceive events from an external perspective, as if they were detached observers. This holistic view allows them to see not only their actions but also their consequences on others.
- **Emotional Aspect:** The life review is not only visual but also emotional. People relive the emotions associated with these events, often with greater intensity than originally experienced. This can include feelings of joy, sadness, regret, love, and other deep emotions.

- **Moral Judgment:** In many accounts, the life review is accompanied by a sense of moral judgment. Individuals feel they are evaluating their actions and decisions based on ethical and moral values. This judgment may occur internally or be perceived as coming from an external presence or higher power.
- **Learning and Growth:** The life review is often described as an opportunity for learning and personal growth. Individuals report gaining a deeper understanding of their actions and their impact on others, leading to greater awareness and, in some cases, positive changes in their lives.

According to Martial and colleagues (2017), the life review is one of the most frequently described elements in near-death experiences. Several studies indicate that individuals who have undergone a life review tend to report significant transformations in their attitudes and subsequent behavior. Many report that this experience changed their view of life, relationships, and their purpose. The awareness of one's actions and their consequences can lead to greater empathy, compassion, and a desire to live more ethically and meaningfully.

Altered Perception of Time in Near-Death Experiences

Altered perception of time is a frequently reported phenomenon in near-death experiences (NDEs) and represents one of the key elements characterizing these experiences. Here is a more in-depth explanation of this phenomenon:

- **Definition and Characteristics:**
  - **Sense of Eternity or Expanded Time:** Many people report that during an NDE, time seems to slow down or stop completely. Some describe the sensation of living an entire life or reviewing past events in mere moments, as if time were dilated. This sense of eternity can make the experience particularly intense and meaningful.

- - **Simultaneous Experiences:** Some individuals report living events simultaneously rather than sequentially. This means that different memories or experiences can be perceived all at once, creating a sensation of merging the past, present, and future.
  - **Accelerated Thinking:** In contrast to the slowing of time, people's thoughts during an NDE can accelerate. They report an extraordinary mental speed, allowing them to think and reflect much faster than normal.
- **Examples of Altered Perception of Time:**
  - **Slowing of Time:** During a car accident, a person might perceive that everything moves in slow motion, allowing them to observe details that they normally would not notice in such a brief situation.
  - **Life Review:** In a matter of seconds, a person might review their entire life, with clear and detailed perceptions of events that happened many years before. This review can include the emotions and sensations felt during those moments, all condensed into a short span of time.
- **Possible Explanations:**
  - **Physiological:** Some researchers suggest that altered time perception during an NDE might be related to changes in brain processes. During situations of extreme stress or danger, the brain may process information differently, influencing our perception of time.
  - **Psychological:** Time perception is also influenced by emotional states. During an NDE, intense fear, wonder, or other strong emotions can distort time perception, making it seem slowed down or sped up.

- o **Neurochemical:** Changes in neurotransmitter levels, such as dopamine, during moments of acute stress can influence time perception. Studies suggest that dopamine plays a crucial role in modulating our temporal perception.

Sensory Amplification in Near-Death Experiences

Sensory amplification is a phenomenon frequently reported in near-death experiences (NDEs). This phenomenon manifests as an intensification of sensory perceptions, making the experience particularly vivid and memorable. Here is a more detailed explanation of this phenomenon:

- **Definition and Characteristics:**
    - o **Vision:** Many people report extraordinarily clear and detailed vision during an NDE. They describe colors as more vivid and contours as sharper than normal vision. Some even perceive things that would normally be outside their field of view, such as 360-degree vision.
    - o **Hearing:** People may perceive sounds with unusual clarity and purity. Music, voices, or ambient sounds are described as extremely detailed and melodious, even if they may not come from a physical source.
    - o **Smell and Taste:** Although less common, some people report amplified smells and tastes during an NDE. They may perceive floral scents, the smell of food, or other aromas with greater intensity than usual.
    - o **Touch:** Tactile sensation can become incredibly acute, with people describing heightened sensitivity to temperature, pressure, or the texture of objects. Some report sensations of lightness or the feeling of floating in the air.
- **Examples of Sensory Amplification:**

- **Extraordinary Vision:** A person during an accident might report seeing every detail of the surrounding environment with surprising clarity, noticing minute details such as the leaves on a tree or the folds in people's clothes.
- **Intensified Hearing:** During a medical crisis, someone might hear their own heartbeat, the noise of medical machines, and the voices of doctors with crystal clarity, even perceiving sounds that they would not normally notice.

- **Possible Explanations:**
    - **Physiological:** During situations of extreme stress or danger, the body releases a cascade of hormones like adrenaline. This can temporarily increase sensory sensitivity as a survival mechanism, allowing greater awareness of the surrounding environment.
    - **Neurochemical:** Changes in neurotransmitter levels can influence sensory perception. For example, elevated levels of dopamine can intensify sensory perceptions, making experiences more vivid and detailed.
    - **Psychological:** The emotional state during an NDE can amplify sensory perceptions. Fear, wonder, or curiosity can make sensations more intense and memorable.
    - **Cognitive:** The brain, in crisis situations, might allocate more cognitive resources to sensory processing, enhancing the ability to perceive and remember sensory details.

Encounter with a Mystical Presence in Near-Death Experiences

The encounter with a mystical presence is a common element in near-death experiences (NDEs) and represents a fascinating and deeply significant aspect for those who experience it. This phenomenon involves the perception of entities or figures that may be interpreted as spiritual guides, deceased relatives, or transcendent beings. Here is a detailed and in-depth explanation of this phenomenon:

- **Definition and Characteristics:**
    - **Nature of the Encounter:** During an NDE, people often report encountering figures they perceive as mystical or spiritual. These figures can vary from beings of light, angels, religious figures, to deceased relatives or friends.
    - **Appearance and Behavior:** The entities encountered can appear in various forms, but they are usually described as benevolent and reassuring figures. They may communicate through words, telepathy, or simply through their comforting presence.
    - **Messages and Interactions:** Interactions with these figures often include receiving messages of comfort, love, or instructions. These encounters can provide a sense of peace and reassurance, reducing the fear of death.
- **Examples of Mystical Encounters:**
    - **Spiritual Guide:** A person during cardiac arrest might see a luminous figure guiding them through a tunnel, communicating that it is not yet their time to die and that they must return.
    - **Deceased Relative:** Someone in a coma might recount speaking with a deceased parent, who told them not to worry and that they still have important things to do on Earth.
- **Possible Explanations:**

- **Neurobiological:** Some neuroscientists suggest that the encounter with mystical figures during an NDE might be the result of abnormal brain activity in regions responsible for visual perception and memory. During extreme stress, the brain might generate these images as a way to find comfort.
- **Psychological:** From a psychological perspective, the encounter with mystical figures can be interpreted as a manifestation of the human need to find meaning and comfort in crisis situations. Mystical figures may represent collective archetypes or manifestations of our deepest hopes and fears.
- **Spiritual:** Many people interpret these encounters as authentic spiritual experiences. In this context, mystical figures are seen as real entities that exist in a dimension beyond the physical world and interact with us in moments of transition or crisis.
- **Cultural:** The form and identity of mystical figures may be influenced by the cultural and religious beliefs of the person experiencing the NDE. For example, Christians might see angelic figures or Jesus, while Buddhists might encounter bodhisattva figures.

Reflections and Implications of the Research

Martial and colleagues' study highlighted the clinical importance of interviewing ICU patients to explore any memories of near-death experiences (NDEs) they may have had during their stay. This approach is valuable not only for understanding the psychological impact an ICU stay can have but also for providing appropriate follow-up care for such patients.

The longitudinal study by Martial and colleagues is pioneering in its exploration of the phenomenological characteristics of memory and the impact of NDEs in ICU survivors. Interestingly, some common NDE characteristics, such as out-of-body experiences and intense feelings of peace, were less frequent in this context compared to other studies.

The research found that a significant portion of the sample had subjective experiences that, while not classified as NDEs according to the Greyson scale, included some typical NDE characteristics. One month after ICU discharge, patients who had experienced an NDE reported a high number of persistent phenomenological characteristics in their memory. The richness of these memories is consistent with existing literature, suggesting that NDEs are characterized by particularly vivid and clear memories. According to Martial and colleagues, this phenomenon could be explained by the release of specific neurotransmitters during critical situations, which enhance the encoding and consolidation of such memories.

In the one-year follow-up, most patients had not significantly changed their opinion about death. This result contrasts with previous research suggesting that NDEs generally lead to a reduced fear of death. Such a discrepancy could be attributed to individual differences in the subjective interpretation of NDEs or the prolonged ICU stay of the patients.

The study also revealed that NDE survivors reported a significant positive impact on self-acceptance and an increased sense of the importance of love. However, the impact on other aspects of life, such as well-being and lifestyle, showed mixed results. This underscores the need for further research to better understand the long-term implications of NDEs.

Several limitations were acknowledged in Martial and colleagues' study. First, the monocentric nature of the study and the limited number of patients who experienced NDEs must be considered. Second, the use of scales with closed-ended questions to identify NDEs, although rigorous, provides a limited understanding of NDEs themselves. The timing of memory assessment (one month after ICU discharge) and the lack of an assessment of cognitive and memory impairments at the time of the interviews are additional limitations.

Conclusion

The study provides valuable insights into the phenomenological characteristics of memory and the impact of NDEs in ICU survivors. The findings highlighted the persistence and vividness of NDE memories and their impact on subjective perceptions of death and psychological well-being. Given the potential psychological implications of experiences during intensive care, the study's authors emphasize the importance of conducting systematic interviews with all survivors to explore any memories and provide appropriate follow-up care.

Exploring near-death experiences among ICU survivors offers a unique window into the human psyche and our understanding of consciousness. As we continue to investigate these phenomena, it is crucial to approach the subject with scientific rigor and an open mind. The journey to understand what awaits us beyond life is as much a matter of scientific inquiry as it is of personal and collective introspection.

References

Martial C, et al. Int J Health Clin Psychol. 2024. Phenomenological memory characteristics and impact of near-death experience in critically ill survivors: Observations at discharge and after a 1-year follow-up.
DOI: *10.1016/j.ijchp.2024.100478.*

Rousseau AF, et al. Incidence of near-death experiences in patients surviving a prolonged critical illness and their long-term impact: a prospective observational study. Crit Care. 2023 Feb 27;27(1):76. doi: 10.1186/s13054-023-04348-2.

Chapter 7: Struck by Fate: A Symphony from the Beyond

It was a beautiful August day in 1994 at Sleepy Hollow Lake, in Athens, New York. The occasion was the annual group birthday celebration for my in-laws. About twenty relatives, including their siblings, were present. While the children ran around wildly, screaming and playing, I was preparing the barbecue for the party. We had gathered on the second floor of a pavilion by the lake, with picnic tables and barbecue areas on the ground floor. A public payphone was attached to the side wall of the building.

As I considered calling my mother to check on her, I remember noticing a few light raindrops. In the midst of the party and chaos, without me realizing it, the beautiful sunny day had given way to powerful storm clouds rapidly moving over the lake.

I approached the payphone and dialed my mother's number. I let the phone ring eight times, but there was no answer. With my left hand, I pulled the receiver away from my face to hang up. When it was about a foot away, I heard a deafening crackle. Simultaneously, I saw a flash of bright light shoot out from the receiver I was holding. A powerful lightning strike had hit the pavilion, traveled through the phone, and struck me in the face, as its massive electrical charge sought a path to the ground.

This is the account of a physician, published by himself in the following case report: Cicoria T, Cicoria J. *Getting comfortable with near-death experiences. My near-death experience: a telephone call from God.* Mo Med. 2014 Jul-Aug;111(4):304-7.

This extraordinary testimony provides a unique insight into near-death experiences, exploring the boundaries of our understanding of life and death. The event described is not just a detailed account of an incredible incident but also a reminder of the fragility of our existence and the possibility of contact with the beyond, which challenges rational explanations.

Personal Reflections

One of the most fascinating aspects surrounding near-death experiences (NDEs) and out-of-body experiences (OBEs) is their scientific explanation. In the case report presented here, a physician and scientist shares his personal story of experiencing events while he was presumably dead. Here's what the physician recounts in the case report mentioned above:

"The force of the lightning strike flung me backward like a rag doll. Despite the tremendous physical trauma, I realized that something strange and incomprehensible was happening. While my body was being hurled back, I felt 'myself' moving forward. Yet, I seemed to be still and confused, staring at the phone that hung in front of me. Nothing made sense.

At that moment, I heard my mother-in-law scream from the top of the stairs above me. She rushed down toward me. I felt like a deer caught in headlights. As she approached, I saw her looking beyond me, to my right, and she headed in that direction. She was completely unaware of my presence. I turned to see where she was going. Suddenly, I realized what was happening. A motionless body lay on the ground about ten feet behind me. To my astonishment, another look confirmed that it was me!

I watched a woman who had been waiting to use the phone kneel down and begin administering CPR. I spoke to the people around my body, but they couldn't see or hear me; I could see and hear everything they did and said. Suddenly, I became aware that I was thinking normal thoughts, with the same mental vernacular I had always possessed. At that moment, I had a simple, inelegant, and crude thought: 'Holy crap, I'm dead.'

This cosmic realization of consciousness meant that my self-awareness was no longer in the lifeless body on the ground. I, whatever I was now, was capable of thought and reasoning. Curiously, there was no strong emotion accompanying my apparent death. I was shocked, sure, but otherwise, I felt no reaction to what should have been the most emotionally charged event of my life.

Seeing no reason to stay with my body, my thoughts shifted toward leaving. I turned and began to ascend the stairs where I knew my family was still gathered. As I started up the steps, I looked at the stairs as I normally would. I saw that, by the third step, my legs began to dissolve. I remember being disturbed by the fact that, by the time I reached the top of the stairs, I had completely lost form and had become only a sphere of energy and thought. My mind raced frantically, trying to record and make sense of what was happening.

At the top of the first flight of stairs, the stairs turned left into the second flight. Instead of dealing with the stairs, I passed through the wall into the room where everyone was. I floated diagonally across the room, above my wife who was painting the children's faces. She had a child in front of her, one behind her, and one to her left. I had a clear realization that my family would be fine. Without emotion, I left the building.

Once outside, I was immersed in a blue-white light that had a shimmering quality, as if I were swimming underwater, in a crystal-clear stream. Sunlight penetrated it. The vision was accompanied by a feeling of absolute love and peace.

What does 'absolute love and peace' mean? For example, scientists use the term absolute zero to describe a temperature where no molecular movement exists, a singular and pure state. That was what I felt; I had fallen into a purely positive energy stream. I could see the flow of this energy. I could see it moving through the fabric of everything. I reasoned that this energy was quantifiable. It was something measurable and tangible. As I floated in the current of this stream, which seemed to have both speed and direction, I saw some of the highs and lows of my life flash by, but nothing in depth. I became ecstatic at the possibility of where I was heading. I was aware of every moment of this experience, conscious of every millisecond, even though I could feel that time didn't exist. I remember thinking, 'This is the greatest thing that could ever happen to anyone.'

Suddenly, I found myself back in my body. It was so painful. My mouth burned, and my left foot hurt... it felt as if someone had driven a hot iron into my ankle. I was still unconscious, but I could feel the woman who had been doing CPR stop and kneel beside me. It seemed like an eternity before I could open my eyes. I wanted to tell her, 'Thank you for helping me.' Absurdly, all I could manage to say was, 'It's okay, I'm a doctor.'

Shortly after regaining consciousness, the camp's security arrived and insisted on calling an ambulance, but I stubbornly refused, much to their frustration. Although I realized I probably didn't make much sense, the truth about lightning strikes is that you're either dead or alive, and there's not much in between. In hindsight, it's clear I wasn't thinking clearly, but at the time, I was still overwhelmed by what I had just experienced. My family drove me home to Oneonta, NY, a two-and-a-half-hour trip, during which I was groggy and disoriented. Once there, I consulted my cardiologist and a local neurologist who performed all the necessary tests and examinations. They merely told me how lucky I was to still be alive.

I was able to return to work two weeks after the initial lightning strike when my brain seemed to be functioning normally again. However, in the weeks and months following the strike, I changed in many ways. What happened to my musical ability in developing and composing music after that event, I have discussed in various books and documentaries."

This account is not just a detailed recollection of an incredible incident but also a reminder of the fragility of our existence and the possibility of contact with the beyond that defies rational explanations.

Reflections of the Case Report Author

Tony Cicoria recounts experiencing what Raymond Moody, MD, has described as an out-of-body experience (OBE). He refers to this phenomenon as an ND/OBE (near-death out-of-body experience). In his case report, Cicoria focuses primarily on the experiential aspect of ND/OBEs and attempts to apply scientific reasoning to what might elude explanations based on our current knowledge.

As a physician and scientist, he considers it extremely important to attempt a logical explanation of what happened and to examine what he experienced on that fateful day. However, as an individual, he also believes it's equally important to appreciate the indescribable miracle he went through. He had been presumed dead on the ground but was later able to see and verify events that had occurred around him and, in another room, where it would have been physically impossible for him to see. Both aspects are essential in reaching a valid conclusion about this enigmatic event.

His friend and colleague, the renowned neurologist and author Oliver Sacks, MD, assured him that he was having hallucinations… but was he really? Dr. Sacks described hallucinations associated with "ecstatic" seizures in temporal lobe epilepsy, which certainly seem similar to some descriptions of people who have had true NDEs.

However, numerous accounts have been presented and verified in which NDE/OBE subjects have been able to describe in minute visual and auditory detail their experiences. A flagship case is that of Pam Reynolds, described in the book by Michael Sabom, MD, *Light and Death*, and further studied by Holden and Woerlee. Reynolds was a patient who had a NDE/OBE during a neurosurgical procedure called "standstill," devised by Robert Spetzler, MD, at the Barrow Neurological Institute. This procedure was used during the resection of a brain aneurysm, during which the patient's heart was stopped and the brain was isoelectric and unresponsive. Just before the standstill procedure began, Reynolds was deeply anesthetized, with her eyes taped shut and a sheet over her head. Her brain activity was monitored in multiple ways to confirm that the anesthesia was complete; yet, she described "bursting" out of her body, having a ND/OBE during which she could describe sounds, "see" where people were positioned, and describe the shape of surgical instruments used on her, which she physically could not have seen.

Dr. Gerald Woerlee argues that she might have had moments of light anesthesia, which can certainly happen in surgery, but this would only allow auditory recognition, not visual. She was able to mimic the sound of a brutal instrument called the Midas Rex, used to saw open her skull. More importantly, she was able to accurately describe its appearance in lay terms.

Pim van Lommel, a Dutch cardiologist, conducted a prospective study on 344 cardiac arrest patients, finding that 18% of them had experienced a NDE/OBE (Van Lommel, 2001; 2010; 2011). In other studies, the percentage of such phenomena in cardiac arrest survivors who recalled a NDE or OBE was quite variable. Melvin Morse (Morse, 1996), for example, described a percentage of 85% in children. According to Kenneth Ring (Ring, 1999), even blind people have reported NDE/OBE episodes, describing accurate perceptions impossible to have from their physical body's position, and sometimes contrary to expectations.

These examples demonstrate that ND/OBEs are not mere hallucinations but complex phenomena that deserve thorough scientific investigation. Tony Cicoria's testimony, along with documented cases like Pam Reynolds', suggests that there are aspects of human consciousness and perception that still elude our understanding. Ongoing research in this field could lead to new discoveries that challenge current scientific explanations and open the door to a deeper understanding of the human mind and its capacity to experience realities beyond the physical world.

What Do Skeptics Say?

Skeptics attribute near-death experiences (NDEs) to a dying brain or hallucinations, pointing to studies that simulate similar experiences through stimulation of certain brain areas (Cicoria et al., 2014). Wilder Penfield was one of the first to physically stimulate the brain in some patients (Penfield, 1958), while Olaf Blanke (Blanke et al., 2004) demonstrated that the temporal lobe and amygdala might be involved. Jimo Borjigin (Borjigin et al., 2013) and Chawla (Chawla et al., 2009) studied brain activity following cardiac arrest, suggesting that a transient surge of high-frequency gamma oscillations precedes brain death, hypothesizing that this mechanism might explain NDEs. However, cases of plausible experiences documented after clinical death remain unexplained.

The idea that consciousness may survive death is not new, with references dating back to Plato and Pythagoras. While there are connections between the brain and these experiences, real-life changes following episodes of NDE/OBE, in which people verify details they could not have known, cannot simply be explained as cases of "anoxia" (sudden lack of oxygen to the brain) or as hallucinations (Cicoria et al., 2014).

For many, as in the story of this physician, consciousness may survive death, suggesting that life is greater than the sum of its parts—an idea echoed in the words of Robin Kelly, who stated that "Our brain may not be the seat of consciousness, but simply a vessel through which consciousness is realized."

Further studies and research could help corroborate what many who have experienced near-death already know: that the gift of life is greater than the sum of its parts and that, whatever consciousness may be, it survives death.

References

Blanke O, et al. Out of body experience and autoscopy of neurological origin. Brain 2004;127(2):243–258.

Borjigin J, et al. Surge of neurophysiological coherence and connectivity in the dying brain. PNAS. 2013;110(35):14432–14437.

Cicoria T, et al. Getting comfortable with near-death experiences. My near-death experience: a telephone call from God. Mo Med 2014 Jul-Aug;111(4):304-7.

Chawla L, et al. Surges of EEG activity at the time of death: a case series. J Palliative Med 2009;12(12):1095–1100.

Morse M. Parting Visions: a New Scientific Paradigm. In: Baily LW, Yates J, editors. The Near Death Experience: a Reader. New York and London: Routledge, 1996, pp. 299–318.

Holden J. Personal communication. 2013, 2014.

Penfield W. *The Excitable Cortex in Conscious Man.* Liverpool: Liverpool University Press, 1958.

Ring K, et al. *Mindsight: Near Death and Out of Body Experiences in the Blind.* Palo Alto: William James Center for Consciousness Studies, 1999.

Sacks O. Seeing God in the Third Millennium. How the Brain Creates Out of Body Experiences and Religious Epiphanies. *The Atlantic.* 2012 Dec;1–7.

Sabom M. *Light and Death: One Doctor's Fascinating Account of Near Death Experiences.* Grand Rapids, Michigan: Zondervan Publishing House, 1998

Van Lommel P, et al. Near Death Experience in Survivors of Cardiac Arrest: a Prospective Study in the Netherlands. *Lancet* 2001;58:2039–2045.

Van Lommel P. *Consciousness Beyond Life: the Science of the Near Death Experience.* New York: Harper-Collins, 2010.

Van Lommel P. Near Death experiences: the experience of the self as real and not as an illusion. *ANYAS* 2011;1234:19–28.

Woerlee G. Could Pam Reynolds Hear? A New Investigation into the Probability of Hearing during this Famous Near Death Experience. *J Near Death Studies* 2011;30(1):3–25.

Chapter 8: A Case of Septic Shock in Obstetrics

Obstetric shock (OS) is one of the leading causes of maternal mortality worldwide. Surviving severe forms of OS poses a significant risk of chronic morbidity, both somatic and psychological, due to the consequences of multi-organ failure that occurs in such conditions (Habek, 2018).

Obstetric shock is a medical emergency that occurs during childbirth or in the postpartum period and can be caused by various conditions, including hemorrhage, infections, amniotic fluid embolism, or preeclampsia. This condition can lead to multi-organ failure and, if not treated promptly, can be fatal.

We recount, in the words of the authors of a scientific article published in 2022 (Habek et al., 2022), a clinical case:

"The patient, a healthy 28-year-old primipara, developed severe acute postpartum hemorrhage following a spontaneous delivery due to uterine atony, with disseminated intravascular coagulation and severe Grade IV hypovolemic obstetric shock, leading to loss of consciousness. Just before losing consciousness, the patient said that she was going to die.

All resuscitation measures were promptly implemented: endotracheal intubation with assisted breathing and oxygenation, intravascular volume replenishment with crystalloids, colloids, and blood products, along with inotropic drugs, atropine, epinephrine, dopamine, dobutamine, manual exploration, and compression of the uterus by an anesthesiologist, two gynecologists, and three midwives.

A senior consultant was called to perform hemostatic sutures and uterine tamponade. After this intervention, the bleeding stopped, and blood loss was estimated at over three and a half liters, consistent with the patient's severe obstetric shock.

Treatment continued in the intensive care unit, providing respiratory support, intensive therapy, and monitoring. During the resuscitation procedure in the delivery room, the woman was unconscious, never having been sedated or anesthetized. Her personal and family history was devoid of psychiatric data or religious fanaticism.

Two days after treatment in the intensive care unit, during contact with the doctors, the patient detailed what had happened to her in the delivery room with the following words: 'I saw a bright light and from above, I observed all the events that were very dramatic, but I didn't feel uncomfortable. I saw my pale body lying there with a tube in my mouth, and a doctor inflating a bag for artificial respiration.

My legs were covered in blood, and the floor was soaked with it. Another doctor arrived, put on an apron, sat between my legs, vigorously pushed large pieces of gauze into my uterus, and said that a hysterectomy couldn't be performed on a woman in that condition.

He asked what the blood test results were, and the doctor inflating the bag said that the patient wasn't clotting and was bleeding, that there was no blood pressure or pulse. Nurses and doctors were pumping blood and infusions from plastic bags hanging on a stand.

After the bleeding stopped, I was transferred from the delivery room to the transport stretcher for the intensive care unit. The entire room was covered in my blood, and the sheets were soaked with blood, and my awareness of what was happening ended.'

'You are the doctor who saved my life,' she added, addressing a senior consultant she could not have seen before, as she had already lost consciousness and been intubated. 'Thank you,' she said to the doctors."

This extraordinary account provides a unique insight into near-death experiences and the psychological and physical impact of obstetric shock. The patient's testimony is not only a detailed account of an incredible medical incident but also a reminder of the fragility of our existence and the possibility of contact with the beyond that challenges rational explanations.

An Integrated Approach to Near-Death Experiences in the Context of Obstetric Shock

As the author of the case report argues, the surprising experience described demonstrates that out-of-body experiences (OBEs) can occur in moments of crisis when the body is on the brink between life and death. The scientific interpretations of near-death experiences (NDEs) and OBEs vary, ranging from neurological explanations to spiritual ones. In the case of the patient, her experience remains a mystery, a testament to how consciousness can, under extreme circumstances, separate from the body.

Certainly, several near-death experiences have been described in obstetric cases involving cardiac arrest, obstetric embolisms, severe forms of obstetric shock, or sudden clinical death. However, the authors have described such a case for the first time, adding a significant contribution to the existing literature.

The author's analysis contributes to the evident existence of this phenomenon, which cannot be attributed to any psychiatric pathology. The relationship between severe Grade IV obstetric shock, multi-organ failure, insufficient cerebral perfusion, and NDE is particularly interesting.

This phenomenon is particularly fascinating because it highlights how the original translation of the word "resuscitation"—re + anima (repeated return of the soul or spirit, according to the ancient medicine of Hippocrates and Galen)—can have a realistic interpretation in medical situations like the one described.

In the case of this patient, her near-death experience and out-of-body episode during severe obstetric shock and subsequent resuscitation represent a vivid example of how consciousness can separate from the body in critical situations. It is reported that such experiences are accompanied by sensations of peace, tranquility, and detachment from physical reality, indicating a phenomenon that goes beyond the simple physiological response of the brain to life-threatening situations.

These observations raise crucial questions about the nature of consciousness and the possibility that it may exist independently of the physical body. Further studies and research could contribute to a deeper understanding of these phenomena, offering new perspectives not only in medicine but also in the philosophy of mind and spirituality.

Personal Reflections on the Case Report

Near-death experiences (NDEs) in the context of obstetric shock are a fascinating phenomenon that raises important questions about the nature of consciousness and life itself. On the one hand, these experiences can be interpreted as a product of the brain's physiology under extreme conditions, such as hypoxia or multi-organ failure. On the other hand, they suggest the possibility that consciousness may exist independently of the body, as proposed by ancient medical and philosophical traditions.

Personally, I believe it is essential to approach these experiences with an open mind and a balanced approach, recognizing the value of both scientific explanations and spiritual interpretations. NDEs offer a unique and potentially transformative insight into the human condition, highlighting the complexity of the mind and the depth of human experience.

It is important to remember that what cannot be proven today with current scientific tools may be provable tomorrow. The scientific method is based on the principle of falsifiability, as suggested by the philosopher of science Karl Popper, who argued that a theory is scientific only when it is "falsifiable." This means that science is an ever-evolving process, always open to new discoveries and reinterpretations of what is already known.

Rather than attempting to reduce NDEs to a mere physiological phenomenon or, conversely, idealizing them as transcendental experiences, we should adopt an integrated approach that embraces both science and spirituality. In this way, we can develop a more comprehensive understanding of NDEs and, more broadly, of the nature of human existence, fostering greater awareness and appreciation of the mystery and beauty of life.

Recent Medical Discoveries on Consciousness and NDEs

In recent years, scientific research on consciousness has led to numerous discoveries, helping us better understand the different forms of consciousness and their relationship to near-death experiences (NDEs). Recent studies have shown that consciousness can be divided into different components, such as wakefulness, the relationship with the external environment, and internal awareness. While wakeful consciousness is characterized by a state of alertness and the ability to interact with the external world, internal awareness represents a form of consciousness focused on thoughts, memories, and internal perceptions.

During NDEs, even though wakefulness and connection with the external environment are interrupted, internal awareness can remain intact. This phenomenon, known as "disconnected consciousness," has been studied as a particular form of consciousness that occurs when a person is unaware of the external environment but aware of their own thoughts and feelings (Martial et al., 2020).

NDEs have been associated with states of "altered" or "non-ordinary" consciousness, characterized by unique cognitive, emotional, and mystical experiences. In these states, people may experience vivid memories, sensations of peace, or out-of-body experiences. This type of consciousness is often considered a form of "disconnected consciousness," occurring when a person is aware of their thoughts and feelings but not of their surroundings.

These recent developments in understanding consciousness have important implications for the study of NDEs. For example, the distinction between internal and external awareness can help explain how people can experience vivid NDEs while in an apparent unconscious state, such as during a coma or cardiac arrest. Internal awareness can remain active, allowing people to have intense experiences even when they are not aware of their surroundings.

NDEs are often described as experiences of "disconnected consciousness" (Martial et al., 2020), in which people experience internal awareness while being separated from the external environment. This understanding can help distinguish between classic NDEs, which occur in life-threatening situations, and NDE-like experiences, which can occur during meditation or sleep. Additionally, this distinction can facilitate comparisons between NDEs and other forms of disconnected consciousness, such as dreams or drug-induced hallucinations, allowing for a deeper understanding of these phenomena.

These advances in our understanding of consciousness and NDEs not only expand our scientific knowledge but also raise new philosophical and spiritual questions about the nature of consciousness and its ability to exist independently of the physical body. Continuing to explore these experiences with an integrated approach that embraces both science and spirituality brings us closer to a more complete understanding of the human mind and our existence.

References

Martial C, et al. Near-Death Experience as a Probe to Explore (Disconnected) Consciousness. Trends Cogn Sci. 2020 Mar;24(3):173-183. doi: 10.1016/j.tics.2019.12.010. Epub 2020 Jan 22.

Habek D, et al. Near-Death Experiences in Case of Severe Obstetrics Shock. Psychiatr Danub 2022 Fall;34(3):525-526.

Chapter 9: Near-Death Experiences and Sleep

Chapter 9: Near-Death Experiences and Sleep

Near-death experiences (NDEs) are complex and fascinating phenomena that continue to captivate both the scientific and spiritual communities. Defined as conscious perceptual experiences that include emotional, self-related, spiritual, and mystical aspects, NDEs occur in individuals close to death or in situations of imminent physical or emotional threat (Greyson, 1983). Reports of NDEs describe a variety of extraordinary sensations, such as accelerated thought processes, time distortion, out-of-body experiences, and visual and auditory hallucinations (Greyson, 1983; Knoblauch, Schmied & Schnettler, 2001; Van Lommel et al., 2001; Martial et al., 2017; Cassol et al., 2018). Despite extensive research, the pathophysiological basis of these experiences remains largely unknown (Peinkhofer, Dreier & Kondziella, 2019).

An intriguing aspect of NDEs is their phenotypic similarity to experiences that occur during REM (Rapid Eye Movement) sleep. REM sleep is characterized by rapid eye movements, loss of muscle tone, vivid dreams, and cortical activation revealed by EEG desynchronization (Peever & Fuller, 2017). The features of the REM state can intrude into wakefulness, both in healthy individuals and those with narcolepsy, causing visual and auditory hallucinations at sleep onset (hypnagogic) or upon awakening (hypnopompic), as well as muscle atonia with sleep paralysis and cataplexy (Scammell, 2015; Jalal & Ramachandran, 2017; Baird et al., 2018).

The similarity between NDEs and REM sleep experiences raises intriguing questions about the nature of consciousness and the experiences perceived in altered states. Both phenomena exhibit elements of time distortion, intense sensory perceptions, and states of bodily dissociation. This connection suggests that they may share similar neurobiological mechanisms, although the contexts in which they occur differ.

Research on the overlap between NDEs and REM sleep may offer new insights into the understanding of these phenomena. For instance, visual and auditory hallucinations, common in both NDEs and REM intrusions during wakefulness, may arise from abnormal activation of brain areas responsible for sensory processing. Similarly, the out-of-body experience frequently reported in NDEs could be explained through mechanisms akin to those causing sleep paralysis, where the individual is aware but unable to move.

In summary, understanding the similarities between NDEs and REM sleep could provide valuable clues about the nature of consciousness and the neurological processes underlying extraordinary experiences. Continuing to explore these connections with scientific rigor and open-mindedness is essential for advancing our understanding of these fascinating and complex phenomena.

A Case-Control Study on the Relationship Between REM Sleep and Near-Death Experiences

A case-control study found that individuals with near-death experiences (NDEs) reported significantly more REM sleep intrusions than age- and gender-matched controls, suggesting that REM sleep intrusion may contribute to NDEs (Nelson et al., 2006). However, this study has been criticized for various reasons, including selection bias (Long & Janice Miner, 2007). Critics pointed out that the controls, recruited from medical personnel and their contacts, may have been influenced by their medical background.

To further explore this relationship, Kondziella and colleagues (2019) examined the association between REM sleep intrusion and NDEs using a different approach. They recruited a large multinational sample of ordinary people through an online crowdsourcing platform, Prolific Academic. The primary objective was to estimate the frequency of NDEs and REM sleep intrusions in a large sample of adults. The secondary objective was to test the hypothesis that individuals reporting an NDE have a higher frequency of REM sleep intrusions.

The findings of Kondziella and colleagues confirmed that individuals with near-death experiences tend to have more REM sleep intrusions than the general population. This study improved the understanding of NDEs by using a more diverse sample and reducing selection bias. Additionally, the use of a crowdsourcing platform allowed for a more representative sample of the general population, enhancing the validity of the results.

The association between REM sleep intrusions and NDEs raises intriguing questions about the nature and origin of these experiences. One possible explanation is that REM sleep intrusions, which include visual and auditory hallucinations, sleep paralysis, and muscle atonia, may influence the perception and interpretation of NDEs. In other words, the altered states of consciousness typical of REM sleep may contribute to creating the extraordinary experiences that characterize NDEs.

However, it is important to note that while there is a correlation between REM sleep intrusions and NDEs, this does not necessarily imply a direct causality. Further research is needed to determine whether REM sleep intrusions are a predisposing factor or simply a phenomenon associated with NDEs.

Study Findings

Kondziella and colleagues recruited 1,034 individuals from 35 countries, most of whom resided in Europe and North America. Two hundred eighty-nine participants (28%) claimed to have had a near-death experience (NDE), with 106 reaching the threshold of 7 or more points on the Greyson Near Death Experience Scale (GNDES). The situations in which these experiences occurred varied widely, including car accidents, near-drownings, substance abuse, and childbirth complications.

NDEs were often accompanied by symptoms such as abnormal time perception, exceptionally rapid thought processes, vivid senses, and sensations of separation from the body. Interestingly, about one-third of the participants who reported an NDE claimed to have had two or three such experiences.

Association Between Near-Death Experiences and REM Sleep Intrusion

The study confirmed a significant association between NDEs and REM sleep intrusion. After multivariate analysis, REM sleep intrusion remained the only factor significantly correlated with NDEs. This finding supports the data from the previous study by Nelson et al., suggesting that REM sleep intrusions may explain much of the semiology of NDEs.

The anonymity of the online survey avoided the selection bias present in previous studies. Kondziella and colleagues carefully adjusted for confounding factors such as age, gender, place of residence, and perception of danger, finding that the association between NDEs and REM sleep intrusion remained highly significant.

Discussion

Using crowdsourcing methods, Kondziella and colleagues found that one in ten people had experienced a confirmed NDE. This figure is slightly higher than previously reported but confirms the association between NDEs and REM sleep intrusion. Although the association does not imply causality, identifying the physiological mechanisms behind REM sleep intrusion during wakefulness could advance our understanding of near-death experiences.

Conclusion

Kondziella and colleagues' study confirmed that near-death experiences are common phenomena and that there is a significant association with REM sleep intrusion. Identifying the physiological mechanisms underlying this intrusion could offer new insights into the physiology of near-death experiences, contributing to a deeper understanding of these fascinating phenomena.

References

Cassol H, et al. Qualitative thematic analysis of the phenomenology of near-death experiences. PLOS ONE. 2018;13(2):e0193001 DOI 10.1371/journal.pone.0193001

Greyson B. The near-death experience scale. Construction, reliability, and validity. The Journal of Nervous and Mental Disease. 1983;171:369–375

Knoblauch H, et al. Different kinds of near-death experience: a report on a survey of near-death experiences in Germany. Journal of Near-Death Studies. 2001;20:15–29 DOI 10.1023/A:1011112727078

Kondziella D, et al. Prevalence of near-death experiences in people with and without REM sleep intrusion. PeerJ. 2019 Aug 27;7:e7585. doi: 10.7717/peerj.7585.

Chapter 10: A Systematic Review of Clinical Cases of NDEs

Chapter 10: A Systematic Review of Clinical Cases of NDEs

Near-death experiences (NDEs) are complex and fascinating phenomena that involve individuals who are either on the brink of death or have temporarily crossed the threshold of death. These experiences, often characterized by transcendental elements, frequently lead to profound and lasting changes in both the personal and social lives of those who have undergone them.

In this chapter, I would like to present the findings of a recent systematic review of the literature, conducted by Hashemi and colleagues (2023). The aim of this study was to examine near-death experiences in individuals with diverse religious and cultural backgrounds.

The analysis was conducted systematically, including all case reports, case series, and qualitative research studies documenting NDEs in patients, without any language restrictions, and covering the period from 1980 to 2022. The study followed the guidelines for systematic reviews set forth by the Joanna Briggs Institute (JBI) and the PRISMA-P 2015 checklist. The results were synthesized and evaluated using the "JBI Critical Appraisal Checklist."

A total of 2,407 studies were identified, of which 54 were included in the final analysis. These studies involved 465 individuals who had experienced a near-death episode. Among these studies, 27 were case reports, 20 were case series, and 7 were qualitative studies. The authors categorized the NDEs into four main categories and 19 subcategories. The main categories included emotional, cognitive, spiritual and religious, and supernatural experiences.

The analysis revealed that the most common NDEs were those of a supernatural nature, particularly the experience of leaving the body (Out-of-Body Experience, OBE). Despite differences in interpretations and explanations, these experiences shared a common core, such as the sensation of being outside the body, passing through a tunnel, heightened senses, and similar phenomena. According to the authors, recognizing this common core is essential for providing meaningful responses to patients.

In many studies, supernatural perceptions included involuntary passage through a tunnel, movement toward the ceiling, viewing one's physical body from above (a phenomenon known as bilocation), awareness of distant places from the body, and the ability to pass through physical objects like walls.

Emotional experiences were divided into two subcategories: positive and negative experiences. Positive experiences, such as the absence of fear and a sense of peace and tranquility, were the most common. Negative experiences, on the other hand, included feelings of distress, fear, and torment.

Cognitive experiences were categorized into four subcategories: changes in time perception, increased awareness, life review, and changes in understanding. Many participants reported perceiving time as slowing down or speeding up, while others described heightened awareness and a clear vision of their life.

Spiritual and religious experiences were divided into four subcategories: encounters with spiritual beings, communication with the deceased, visions of otherworldly realms, and the perception of a divine presence.

Hashemi and colleagues' review highlighted that NDEs are characterized by common elements, such as out-of-body experiences and the passage through a tunnel. The differences among various experiences are largely linked to the interpretation and explanation of these phenomena, influenced by individual, cultural, and religious factors. Supernatural experiences were found to be the most common, followed by positive emotional experiences.

These findings suggest that NDEs have a significant impact on individuals' lives, often leading to positive changes such as increased spirituality and a decreased fear of death. However, these experiences can also be traumatic, underscoring the need to provide adequate support to patients who have experienced them.

In summary, this systematic review offers a clearer understanding of NDEs, emphasizing the importance of recognizing supernatural experiences, particularly out-of-body experiences, as a characteristic element. It also underscores the importance of understanding these experiences to provide appropriate support to patients. As is often the case with literature reviews, there remains a need for further research to better understand this phenomenon.

Future Perspectives

Near-death experiences (NDEs) remain a fascinating and mysterious field of research that continues to raise important questions about the nature of consciousness, spirituality, and life itself. The diversity and complexity of these experiences highlight the need for further studies to deepen our understanding of such phenomena. Future studies could focus on various aspects, such as the role of cultural and religious factors, the underlying neurological mechanisms, and the psychological and social impact of NDEs.

One promising area of research involves understanding the brain mechanisms involved in NDEs, which could provide new insights into the functioning of consciousness and the relationship between the brain and mind. This could include the use of advanced neuroimaging techniques to observe brain activity during near-death experiences, as well as comparative studies between individuals who have had NDEs and those who have not.

Additionally, longitudinal studies could examine the long-term impact of NDEs on people's lives, exploring how these experiences influence their perceptions of life, death, and spirituality. Such research could provide valuable information on how NDEs may lead to lasting changes in behavior, beliefs, and interpersonal relationships.

Near-death experiences offer a unique opportunity to explore the boundaries between science and spirituality, paving the way for a deeper and more integrated understanding of the human experience.

The near-death experience is not only a scientific phenomenon but also a profoundly personal and spiritual one. Different religions and cultural traditions offer unique interpretations and perspectives on NDEs, enriching our understanding of this phenomenon.

In the next chapter, we will explore how various world religions approach and interpret near-death experiences, highlighting the similarities and differences in religious and spiritual perspectives on this mysterious phenomenon. We will analyze how cultural and religious beliefs influence the perception and interpretation of NDEs and how these experiences can contribute to a greater understanding of the diversity and universality of human spirituality.

References

Hashemi A, et al. Explanation of near-death experiences: a systematic analysis of case reports and qualitative research. Front Psychol 2023 Apr 20;14:1048929. doi: 10.3389/fpsyg.2023.1048929.

Chapter 11: Near-Death Experiences During Cardiac Arrest

The systematic review conducted by Kovoor et al. (2023) aims to provide a clearer understanding of near-death experiences (NDEs) in patients who have undergone cardiac arrest. Despite decades of study, many aspects of NDEs remain shrouded in mystery, complicated by methodological variations and the intrinsic difficulty of interpreting such deeply personal and profound experiences.

Review Methodology

The methodology employed followed the PRISMA-ScR guidelines (Tricco et al., 2018), with the goal of including only prospective studies that explore NDEs following cardiac arrests. Kovoor's research identified 60 articles, of which 11 were deemed suitable for final analysis. These studies cover a diverse and international population, including research conducted in the United States and Europe (Klemenc-Ketis, 2010, 2011, 2013; Parnia, 2001, 2014, 2023).

Incidence and Variability of NDEs

The review's findings revealed that the incidence of NDEs varies significantly among studies, ranging from a minimum of 6.3% to a maximum of 39.3% (Parnia, 2023), suggesting that up to one-third of resuscitated patients may experience an NDE. This variation is attributable to several factors, including the contexts of the cardiac arrests (in-hospital vs. out-of-hospital) and the methodologies used for detection.

Characteristics and Content of NDEs

The content of NDEs often reflects the language of the questionnaires used rather than the participants' authentic words (Greyson, 1983). Typically, NDEs include sensations of peace, experiences of light, and external visual or auditory awareness. Some studies have reported that patients describe encounters with deceased individuals or luminous, loving entities, as well as a sense of separation from their physical bodies.

Associated Factors and Long-Term Outcomes

Individual variables such as age, the presence of comorbidities, and the characteristics of the cardiac event itself show a significant association with the likelihood of experiencing an NDE. Interestingly, NDEs can positively influence survivors' attitudes toward life and social relationships. However, an analysis revealed higher 30-day mortality in patients with NDEs compared to those without (Van Lommel et al., 2001).

Clinical Implications and Future Research Directions

The research underscores the need to deepen our understanding of NDEs, not only for their immediate clinical implications but also for their potential long-term impact on patients' mental health and well-being. New standards proposed by Parnia et al. (2022) for the study of recalled death experiences aim for greater precision in defining and detecting NDEs, hoping to significantly improve the quality of future research.

Conclusions

Despite methodological and interpretative challenges, near-death experiences continue to offer an important window into some of the most profound and mysterious human experiences. This field of study remains fertile for further investigation, especially regarding the implications of such experiences on consciousness and the very essence of human experience. NDEs invite broader reflection on the meaning of life and death, urging us to explore the boundaries of our understanding of the human mind.

References

Greyson B. The near-death experience scale. J Nerv Mental Dis. 1983;171:369–375. doi: 10.1097/00005053-198306000-00007.

Kovoor JG, et al. Near-death experiences after cardiac arrest: a scoping review. Discov Ment Health. 2024 May 28;4(1):19. doi: 10.1007/s44192-024-00072-7.

Tricco AC, et al. PRISMA extension for scoping reviews (PRISMA-ScR): checklist and explanation. Ann Intern Med. 2018;169:467–473. doi: 10.7326/M18-0850

van Lommel P, et al. Near-death experience in survivors of cardiac arrest: a prospective study in the Netherlands. Lancet. 2001;358:2039–2045. doi: 10.1016/S0140-6736(01)07100-8.

Parnia S, et al. A qualitative and quantitative study of the incidence, features and aetiology of near death experiences in cardiac arrest survivors. Resuscitation. 2001;48:149–156. doi: 10.1016/S0300-9572(00)00328-2.

Parnia S, et al. AWARE-AWAreness during REsuscitation-a prospective study. Resuscitation. 2014;85:1799–1805. doi: 10.1016/j.resuscitation.2014.09.004

Parnia S, et al. Guidelines and standards for the study of death and recalled experiences of death—a multidisciplinary consensus statement and proposed future directions. Ann N Y Acad Sci. 2022;1511:5–21. doi: 10.1111/nyas.14740.

Parnia S, et al. AWAreness during REsuscitation - II: A Multi-Center Study of Consciousness and Awareness in Cardiac Arrest. Resuscitation. 2023:109903.

Klemenc-Ketis Z, et al. The effect of carbon dioxide on near-death experiences in out-of-hospital cardiac arrest survivors a prospective observational study. Crit Care. 2010;14:R56. doi: 10.1186/cc8952.

Klemenc-Ketis Z, et al. Near-death experiences and electrocardiogram patterns in out-of-hospital cardiac arrest survivors. Signa Vitae. 2011;6:31–35. doi: 10.22514/SV62.102011.4

Klemenc-Ketis Z. Life changes in patients after out-of-hospital cardiac arrest : the effect of near-death experiences. Int J Behav Med. 2013;20:7–12. doi: 10.1007/s12529-011-9209-y

Chapter 12: Awareness of the Body During Out-of-Body Experiences

Imagine being able to leave your body and observe yourself from the outside, as if you were watching another person. This phenomenon, known as an out-of-body experience (OBE), offers a unique glimpse into how the brain constructs our perception of the body. While it may seem like science fiction, these experiences have been scientifically studied, helping us to better understand "body self-awareness," our innate ability to feel and recognize our body without consciously thinking about it.

An OBE occurs when a person perceives themselves as being separated from their physical body, observing themselves and the world around them from an external, often elevated, position. This experience can give the impression of "floating" or "flying" outside the body, viewing oneself from a different perspective, sometimes from above.

During an OBE, individuals experience a clear distinction between their "consciousness" or "psychological self" and their physical body. Although they are aware that their body is in a particular location, they feel disconnected, as if positioned elsewhere, observing their body from outside, as if they were two separate entities. This sensation can be accompanied by a very clear vision of themselves and their surroundings. In some cases, people describe seeing and hearing what is happening around their physical body while in this state of separation.

OBEs can occur in various contexts, such as during sleep, anesthesia, moments of intense stress, or they can be induced through meditation practices or the use of psychoactive substances. Although OBEs are often considered mysterious or paranormal phenomena, modern science primarily studies them as neuropsychological events. Research suggests that these experiences may result from unusual interactions or disruptions among neural systems that manage sensory perception, visual processing, and body awareness. Specific conditions that affect brain function, such as injuries or dysfunctions in particular areas, can increase the likelihood of experiencing an OBE (Bourdin et al., 2017).

Despite the extraordinary nature of these experiences, many people who have them describe them as moments of great clarity and intense reality, which can profoundly influence their perception of life and human existence. These episodes can be transformative, leading to changes in self-perception, interpersonal relationships, and worldview.

The Scientific Roots of Out-of-Body Experiences

Studies on OBEs have revealed that these experiences can be triggered by a variety of factors, including neurological, psychological, and physical ones. Brain injuries, temporal lobe epilepsy, and electrical stimulation of the temporo-parietal cortex have all been linked to the induction of OBEs. These factors suggest that the disconnection between the physical body and sensory perception may be due to dysfunctions in brain areas responsible for multisensory integration.

Multisensory integration is the process by which the brain combines information from various senses to create a coherent perception of the body and the surrounding world. When this process is disrupted, as can happen during an OBE, the mind may separate consciousness from the perception of the physical body. This often occurs under extreme circumstances, such as acute stress, trauma, or anesthesia, when the brain may experience altered sensory processing.

Implications of Out-of-Body Experiences

OBEs provide a unique perspective on body awareness and the nature of consciousness. By examining these phenomena, scientists can gain new insights into how the brain creates our perception of body self-awareness and how anomalies in this process can lead to extraordinary experiences.

Moreover, OBEs may have significant clinical implications. Understanding the mechanisms underlying these experiences can help develop new therapeutic approaches for conditions such as post-traumatic stress disorder (PTSD), anxiety, and other trauma-related conditions. Visualization techniques and mindfulness-based therapies, for example, could be adapted to help people manage and integrate their out-of-body experiences.

In conclusion, out-of-body experiences represent a fascinating window into the complexity of the human mind and our perception of the body. While they may seem mysterious or paranormal, OBEs are increasingly understood as neuropsychological events that reflect the brain's extraordinary capacity to create our perception of self and the surrounding world.

How to Classify OBEs?

Out-of-body experiences (OBEs) are intriguing phenomena in which the projection of an observing self (psychological self) seems entirely dissociated from the physical body and is perceived in extra-personal space. During these episodes, the subject perceives themselves and the world from a position distinct from their physical body. These phenomenological states are classified into three main categories:

1. **Disincarnation**: The sensation of being separated from the physical body.

2. **Remote and Elevated Visuo-Spatial Perspective**: The perception of seeing one's body from an external and elevated perspective (egocentric out-of-body perspective).

3. **Astral Projection**: The vision of one's body from an aerial position, sometimes described as astral projection (Blanke et al., 2004; Anzellotti et al., 2011).

OBEs have been associated with various medical and psychological conditions, including brain injuries (particularly in the parietal and temporal regions), psychiatric disorders, intense emotional states such as near-death experiences, substance use, migraines, and epilepsy. However, they are very rarely reported in dissociative identity disorders.

Recent cultural representations, such as the Marvel movie "Dr. Strange" and the OTT series "The Last Hour," have explored this fascinating phenomenon. In these works, characters experience forms of depersonalization, where their parasomatic component leaves the body and is visualized by their self from a third-person perspective, described as astral projection.

OBEs can be understood as a form of dissociation and transpersonal experience. Although there is an abundance of anecdotal evidence, empirical evidence on the connection between dissociation and OBEs is scarce, indicating a lack of deep understanding of this phenomenon (Lahood, 2007). This strange and rare phenomenon is usually reported in organic states, under the influence of substances, and in intense emotional states.

OBEs in the Context of NDEs

Out-of-body experiences (OBEs) that occur during near-death experiences (NDEs) represent some of the most fascinating and studied aspects of these boundary phenomena. Scientifically, OBEs in this context are believed to result from intense neural activity under severe physical and psychological stress, such as during cardiac arrest or near-drowning situations. During these critical moments, the brain may undergo alterations in its normal functioning due to hypoxia (lack of oxygen) or biochemical imbalances, leading to hallucinations and sensory disorientation.

This "disconnection" between self-awareness and the physical body can be interpreted as a defense mechanism of the brain, attempting to distance itself from pain and physical trauma. From a psychological perspective, some theories suggest that OBEs provide psychological comfort in moments of extreme danger, offering an "escape" from the reality of pain and imminent threat.

Moreover, the projection of the self-outside the body may be linked to deep reflections on life and death, often leading individuals to reconsider their values and beliefs about life after death. These experiences, though deeply personal and subjective, offer significant insights into how the human brain copes with and interprets situations of extreme physical and emotional stress.

The Autoscopy Phenomenon

Negative autoscopy is a particularly intriguing and rare phenomenon. Normally, when we look in a mirror or directly at parts of our body, we expect to see them without any issues. However, in cases of negative autoscopy, this does not happen. This phenomenon occurs when a person, despite looking at their body or seeing their reflection in a mirror, cannot perceive their own image. It is as if the body is invisible or absent from that specific visual perception. This is not a vision problem like blindness but rather a malfunction in body perception or in the brain areas that process visual information related to one's body.

This type of experience can be very disconcerting and disorienting, as it contradicts the everyday experience of seeing and recognizing one's body. The causes can vary, ranging from neurological to psychiatric conditions, where the brain's body map may be temporarily altered or disturbed.

Internal autoscopy is a rare and peculiar psychological phenomenon where a person experiences visual hallucinations of their internal organs. In this condition, individuals perceive their organs, such as the heart or lungs, as visible outside their physical body. These visions are not real physical observations but rather perceptions created by the mind. It is as if the veil that normally hides the body's internal processes is lifted, allowing the person to "see" inside themselves in a completely atypical way. These visions can include specific details of the organs or only vague sensations of their presence.

The causes of internal autoscopy are not yet fully understood, but they are thought to be linked to dysfunctions in how the brain processes sensory information and body image. Anomalies in these brain areas may confuse internal signals with external ones, leading to these unusual visual experiences. The condition may be associated with neurological, psychiatric disorders or may manifest following trauma or intense stress.

The "sense of presence" is a phenomenon where a person distinctly feels the physical closeness of someone who is not actually present. Those who experience this sensation may feel as if an invisible person is next to them, sometimes even sensing the sound of footsteps, breathing, or body heat of this imaginary presence. This can happen even in the absence of any direct visual stimulus suggesting the presence of another person. This phenomenon is often described as if someone were literally behind or beside the subject, even though looking around reveals no one. The sensation can be so realistic that many people turn around to check if someone is really there. Although it may seem unsettling, the sense of presence is generally considered an illusion or psychological phenomenon, related to conditions of stress, fatigue, or specific neurological conditions.

True autoscopy is a particular phenomenon among autoscopy experiences, where a person sees a representation of themselves similar to what would appear in a mirror. However, unlike a normal reflection in a mirror, the person does not identify with the reflected image or the spatial position in which the image appears. This means that while the individual may recognize the image as a representation of themselves, they do not perceive that position as the point from which they are actually observing or experiencing the world. It is as if they see a double of themselves, separate from their current consciousness.

This phenomenon can be disorienting because it challenges the normal experience of perceiving one's body and position as an integrated and central unit in sensory experience. True autoscopy is rare and may be associated with specific neurological conditions that alter how the brain processes and integrates sensory information related to one's body and spatial position.

Autoscopic hallucination is a particularly intense form of autoscopic experience, in which a person sees an exact copy of themselves, which may include the face, torso, or entire body, as if reflected in a mirror. However, unlike a normal mirror reflection, this image is an hallucinatory vision: it appears without the presence of a real mirror and can manifest in any visual space around the person. In this experience, the individual can observe their copy with detailed clarity and often has the sense that the mirror image is as real as their physical body. This vision may appear and disappear suddenly and can be so convincing that the person might try to interact with it, perhaps attempting to touch it or speak to it.

Autoscopic hallucination is often related to neurological or psychiatric conditions that affect perception and visual processing in the brain. It has been observed in contexts of great stress, during sleep disorders, or in association with illnesses such as epilepsy or migraines, where abnormalities in the brain may disturb the normal processes of self-perception. This type of experience can be disturbing and disorienting as it challenges the common perception of identity and bodily presence (Mudgal et al., 2021).

Autoscopic experiences represent an area of great interest in neuroscience, offering a unique window into how the brain constructs our perception of the body and reality. Understanding these phenomena not only helps us uncover the mysteries of body self-awareness but can also provide new perspectives for treating neurological and psychological conditions that affect body perception.

References

Bourdin P, et al. A Virtual Out-of-Body Experience Reduces Fear of Death. PLoS One. 2017 Jan 9;12(1):e0169343. doi: 10.1371/journal.pone.0169343.

Mudgal V, et al. Astral Projection: A Strange Out-of-Body Experience in Dissociative Disorder. Cureus. 2021 Aug 9;13(8):e17037. doi: 10.7759/cureus.17037.

Blanke O, et al. Out-of-body experience and autoscopy of neurological origin. Brain. 2004;127:243–258.

Anzellotti F, et al. Autoscopic phenomena: case report and review of literature. Behav Brain Funct. 2011;7:2.

Lahood G. The participatory turn and the transpersonal movement: a brief introduction. ReVision. 2007;29:2–6.

Chapter 13: Perspectives on the Afterlife Across Cultures and Religions

After exploring the scientific evidence and theories surrounding near-death experiences (NDEs), we find ourselves confronted with questions that touch the deepest chords of our existence. What is the true nature of consciousness? Do NDEs suggest the existence of a reality beyond our comprehension? These experiences, vividly described by those who have lived them, challenge the boundaries between science and spirituality, leading us to reflect on what it truly means to "exist." In this and the next chapter, we will explore how different religions interpret these experiences, offering a spiritual perspective that enriches our understanding of the afterlife.

Throughout history, cultures and religions worldwide have grappled with the enigmatic concept of life after death. The continuity of the soul, spirit, or human consciousness after the end of life is a subject that has captured the imagination and offered comfort, hope, and sometimes fear to countless generations. Below, we will examine how some of the world's major religions perceive the afterlife.

The Christian View

Christianity proposes a belief in an afterlife determined primarily by the actions taken and the faith held in God during earthly life. Christians believe that after death, souls are judged by God. Those who have accepted Jesus Christ as their savior are deemed worthy of eternal life in Heaven, a place where they can live in the presence of God. Those who have rejected Him or lived in sin are destined for Hell, a place of punishment and separation from God. The concept of Purgatory, primarily upheld in Roman Catholicism, is an intermediate state where souls undergo a period of suffering and purification necessary to enter Heaven.

Christianity and the Afterlife

Rooted in the teachings of Jesus Christ and the scriptures of the Bible, Christianity has contemplated the mysteries of the afterlife throughout its history. This religion, which has developed over two millennia, encompasses numerous denominations and traditions, offering a complex picture of what happens after life.

Central to Christian faith is the idea that humans face judgment after death. This judgment, pronounced by God, is based on the individual's faith and actions during earthly existence. Emphasizing the redemptive power of Jesus Christ's sacrifice on the cross, Christians believe that accepting Jesus as savior opens the door to eternal life. This salvation is described in the New Testament as being "born again" (John 3:3) or being "saved" (Romans 10:9).

Heaven awaits those who have lived according to God's will and have accepted Jesus' salvation. Described in the Bible with images of streets of gold, crystal-clear rivers, and perpetual light, Heaven represents an eternal place where souls bask in the glory of God, free from suffering and pain. The book of Revelation (21:4) describes it thus: "He will wipe every tear from their eyes. There will be no more death or mourning or crying or pain."

Conversely, Hell is depicted as the final destination for souls who have rejected God's grace and chosen to live in sin. Far from God's presence, it is a realm of punishment and despair. The Bible describes it with images of darkness, fire, and brimstone. However, interpretations vary: some view Hell as eternal separation from God, while others see it as annihilation or a state of soul sleep.

In Roman Catholic doctrine, Purgatory is considered a temporary state of purification for souls destined for Heaven but who need a cleansing process to atone for their sins. This belief is supported by biblical verses that speak of a "trial by fire" (1 Peter 1:7) and the purification of souls (2 Maccabees 12:41-46). Over the centuries, practices such as prayer and indulgences have been associated with the possibility of helping souls in Purgatory to accelerate their journey to Heaven.

Beyond individual salvation, Christianity has a broader eschatological vision. The belief in the second coming of Jesus and the resurrection of the dead is central to Christian doctrine. On

Judgment Day, believers expect the dead to rise and everyone to be judged. This final judgment inaugurates a new era in which a new Heaven and a new Earth are established, free from sin and death.

Across various denominations and forms of Christianity, from Eastern Orthodoxy to Protestantism, different interpretations of the afterlife exist. However, the fundamental principles remain the same, echoing the promise of hope, redemption, and eternal life in Jesus Christ.

In the following sections, we will examine how other religions, including Islam, Hinduism, and Buddhism, interpret the afterlife, highlighting the similarities and differences in religious and spiritual perspectives on this mysterious phenomenon.

The Islamic View

In Islam, the afterlife is a fundamental concept. Muslims believe that after death, individuals are judged by Allah (God). The righteous are guided to Paradise (Jannah), a place of pleasure and abundance, while those who have lived a life contrary to Allah's will are sent to Hell (Jahannam), a place of torment.

Resurrection and Judgment Day

Resurrection is crucial in Islamic faith. On Judgment Day, all will be resurrected to be judged. Islam, one of the world's major monotheistic religions, emphasizes the afterlife and divine judgment that follows death. Rooted in the teachings of the Quran—the sacred book of Islam—and the Hadith—sayings and actions of the Prophet Muhammad—the concepts of death, the afterlife, and divine judgment are intricately woven into the moral and ethical life of a Muslim.

Muslims believe that life on Earth is a test, with actions, intentions, and faith determining one's fate in the afterlife. Everyone is responsible for their actions, and the balance between good and bad deeds is crucial in view of the final judgment.

The Angel of Death and the Grave

It is believed that the Angel of Death (Azrael) takes the soul of the deceased at the time of death. After burial, two angels, Munkar and Nakir, interrogate the deceased about their faith, testing their belief in Allah and the Prophet Muhammad. This period spent in the grave, known as 'Barzakh,' is a transitional phase before Judgment Day.

Judgment Day (Yawm al-Qiyamah)

This monumental day, often mentioned in the Quran, is when all of humanity is resurrected and judged by Allah, from the beginning to the end of time. It is described as a day when the scales of justice are set, and deeds are weighed. The righteous, whose good deeds outweigh the bad, are rewarded, while those who fail the divine test face the consequences.

Paradise (Jannah)

Jannah, often compared to a garden with rivers flowing beneath it, is the ultimate abode for the righteous. It is a realm of eternal bliss, peace, and pleasure. The Quran describes Jannah with images of lush gardens, rivers of milk, wine, honey, and luxurious dwellings. Those in Jannah enjoy the company of their loved ones and the greatest honor of contemplating the face of Allah.

Hell (Jahannam)

Jahannam is described in the Quran as a place of intense suffering, with blazing fire, boiling water, and molten brass. It serves as a place of punishment for those who did not believe, rejected Allah's guidance, and committed grave sins without seeking repentance. However, it is worth noting that Allah's mercy in Islam is considered vast, and many believe that sincere repentance can save a soul from the torment of Jahannam.

Intercession

An important concept in Islamic eschatology is that of intercession. On Judgment Day, it is believed that the Prophet Muhammad and other prophets and martyrs will intercede on behalf of specific individuals, praying to Allah for their forgiveness.

The Eternal Nature of the Afterlife

The afterlife in Islamic belief is eternal. Once souls enter Jannah or Jahannam, they remain there forever, reaping the results of their earthly actions and choices.

In summary, the Islamic view of the afterlife emphasizes the importance of leading a life rooted in faith, righteousness, and good deeds, emphasizing that this world is transient, and that eternal life awaits individuals in the afterlife.

The Buddhist View of the Afterlife and Rebirth

Buddhism, founded in the 5th century BCE by Siddhartha Gautama, commonly known as the Buddha, offers a unique perspective on life, death, and what lies beyond. Instead of a linear conception of life and death, Buddhism presents a cyclical view of existence intricately connected to the law of karma and the quest for enlightenment.

The Cycle of Samsara

At the heart of Buddhist cosmology is the concept of "samsara," the endless cycle of birth, death, and rebirth. This cycle is not necessarily linear, meaning one can be reborn in various realms or states based on the karma accumulated over time. These realms can range from heavenly abodes to hellish states.

Karma and Its Role

Often misunderstood in popular culture, Karma is a Sanskrit term that means "action." In Buddhism, karma refers to intentional actions of the body, speech, and mind. These actions leave an imprint on consciousness, influencing the nature and conditions of subsequent rebirths. Positive actions can lead to rebirth in higher realms, while negative actions can cause a more difficult existence.

The Six Realms of Existence

Traditional Buddhist cosmology speaks of six realms into which one can be reborn: the heavenly realm, the demi-god realm, the human realm, the animal realm, the realm of hungry ghosts, and the hell realm. Each of these realms is characterized by specific experiences and conditions, and rebirth in each is determined by one's karma.

The Importance of the Human Realm

Among the six realms, the human realm is particularly significant. While filled with suffering, it is also considered the most favorable for spiritual practice and the pursuit of enlightenment. Human birth is seen as a rare and precious opportunity to break free from the cycle of samsara.

Nirvana: The End of Suffering

Nirvana, often described as the "extinguishing" of the flames of desire, hatred, and ignorance, is the ultimate goal in Buddhism. Achieving Nirvana means complete liberation from samsara, bringing an end to the cycle of rebirth and the suffering inherent in it. For those who attain Nirvana, there is no more rebirth; they have realized the true nature of existence and are free from all existential bonds.

The Bodhisattva Ideal

Particularly prominent in Mahayana Buddhism is the Bodhisattva ideal: enlightened beings who, out of compassion, delay their complete enlightenment to help all sentient beings achieve liberation. This emphasizes Buddhism's central values of compassion and altruism.

In Summary

The Buddhist view of the afterlife is not centered on a final resting place but rather on the continuous journey of the soul, shaped by karma, until final liberation is achieved. The teachings emphasize the impermanence of life and the importance of ethical living and mindfulness in the quest for enlightenment and freedom from suffering.

The Hindu Perspective on Life, Death, and the Cosmos

Hinduism, one of the oldest religions in the world, is rich in philosophical, theological, and cosmological views. Rooted in a vast array of sacred texts and scriptures, Hinduism offers a multifaceted understanding of life, death, and the ultimate purpose of human existence.

Like Buddhism, Hinduism also believes in the cycle of birth, death, and rebirth, known as samsara. Karma plays a significant role in determining the nature of an individual's rebirth. Moksha is the ultimate goal—the liberation from the cycle of samsara, resulting in union with the universal spirit, Brahman.

Samsara and the Eternity of the Soul

Central to Hindu belief is the notion of "atman," or the individual soul. The atman is eternal and undergoes cycles of birth, life, death, and rebirth, called "samsara." However, this cyclical existence is not infinite; it is governed by the individual's karma and can be transcended through enlightenment.

Karma - The Cosmic Law

'Karma' is the law of cause and effect. Every thought, word, and action has consequences that shape the nature of one's current life and future rebirths. While karma can be seen as a system of cosmic justice, it is impersonal and operates according to natural laws, much like gravity.

The Various Realms of Existence

Hindu cosmology speaks of various realms or "lokas" where souls can reside based on their accumulated karma. From heavenly realms like "Svarga" to lower realms like "Naraka" (similar to hell), these domains offer different experiences, but all are part of the cycle of samsara.

Moksha - The Pursuit of Liberation

The ultimate goal of human existence in Hinduism is to achieve "Moksha," or a state of liberation or self-realization. This is when the atman, having realized its true nature and its unity with the universal spirit or "Brahman," is freed from the cycle of samsara.

Moksha is characterized by a state of eternal bliss, knowledge, and union with the Divine.

Paths to Moksha

Hinduism offers various paths to achieving Moksha. These include "Bhakti" (devotion), "Jnana" (knowledge), "Karma" (right action), and "Dhyana" (meditation). The diversity of paths reflects the religion's recognition of different individual inclinations and temperaments.

Relevance of Scriptures

The major Hindu scriptures, including the Vedas, the Upanishads, the Bhagavad Gita, and the Puranas, provide insights, stories, and guides for understanding the nature of life, the importance of dharma (righteous duty), and the ways to achieve Moksha.

The Guru-Shishya Tradition

Spiritual guidance in Hinduism is also sought through the Guru-Shishya tradition, in which spiritual teachers (Gurus) guide disciples (Shishyas) on their spiritual journey. This mentor-disciple relationship is revered, as the Guru leads the Shishya from ignorance to knowledge.

In Summary

Hinduism views life as a sacred journey, where every challenge and joy is an opportunity for spiritual growth. The dance of creation, preservation, and destruction, as symbolized by the trinity of gods—Brahma, Vishnu, and Shiva—serves as a reminder of the impermanence of life and the eternal nature of the soul. The religion teaches that beyond the illusions of the world (Maya) lies the immutable truth of Brahman, and realizing this truth is the highest purpose of human existence.

The Sikh Perspective on Life, Death, and Spiritual Evolution

Sikhism, founded by Guru Nanak in the 15th century in the Indian subcontinent, combines monotheism with Eastern concepts of karma and reincarnation. Rooted in the teachings of ten successive Gurus and the sacred scripture Guru Granth Sahib, Sikhism offers insights into the journey of the soul, the nature of God, and the purpose of human life.

Sikhs believe in reincarnation, where the soul is born and reborn in various forms of life until liberation is achieved. A person's actions, or "karma," determine the nature of their rebirth. The goal is to merge with the Divine, breaking the cycle of rebirth. Living according to God's will and remembering Him is central to achieving this goal.

Eternal Soul and Transitory Life

At the core of Sikh belief is the idea that while human life is temporary, the soul (atma) is eternal. It passes through cycles of birth and death, much like the Eastern understanding of reincarnation.

Karma and Divine Justice

Sikhs believe in karma, the universal law of cause and effect. Every action, good or bad, has consequences. This accumulated karma influences a person's life circumstances and the nature of subsequent rebirths.

The Cycle of Existence

The soul's journey through various forms of life—from lower organisms to humans—is considered an evolutionary path. Being born as a human is particularly significant, as it is in this form that one has the awareness and capacity to merge with the Divine and achieve liberation.

The Concept of Waheguru

In Sikhism, God is called Waheguru, the Supreme Being or the creator of all. Waheguru is both immanent and transcendent, permeating all of creation while also existing beyond it. Every Sikh aims to cultivate a deep and personal relationship with Waheguru, realizing that the Divine is present in all.

The Path to Liberation

The ultimate goal in Sikhism is to achieve Mukti, or liberation from the cycle of birth and death. This is achieved by living a righteous life, serving the community, and constantly remembering God. The practices of Simran (remembrance) and Sewa (selfless service) are central to this path.

The Five Pillars of Sikhism

To guide Sikhs in their spiritual journey, Guru Nanak established the "Five Ks"—Kesh (uncut hair), Kara (a steel bracelet), Kanga (a wooden comb), Kachera (cotton undergarments), and Kirpan (a ceremonial dagger). These serve as reminders of a Sikh's commitment to faith and their duties to God and the community.

The Role of the Guru

The ten Gurus of Sikhism played a fundamental role in shaping the beliefs and practices of the faith. Their teachings, compiled in the Guru Granth Sahib, serve as a spiritual guide for Sikhs worldwide. The scripture emphasizes the oneness of God, the brotherhood of humanity, and the importance of living a truthful life.

Community and Service

Central to Sikhism is the concept of Sangat (community) and Pangat (community meal). The Gurdwara (Sikh place of worship) is a spiritual center where community members gather for service and devotion. The practice of Langar, or community kitchen, exemplifies Sikh values of selfless service, equality, and communal harmony.

In Summary

Sikhism offers a profound understanding of the interconnectedness of all life, the omnipresence of the Divine, and the importance of a righteous life. It encourages individuals to transcend religious rituals and recognize God in every heart, emphasizing the universality of the divine experience.

The Jewish Perspective on Life After Death

Jewish views on the afterlife are varied, and there is no universally accepted concept. Historically, "Sheol," a place of darkness and silence, was believed to be where the dead resided. Over time, beliefs evolved. Some Jewish interpretations uphold the idea of resurrection on Judgment Day. There is also the belief in the World to Come ("Olam HaBa"), which could be a heavenly realm for the righteous or a future era of peace on Earth.

Judaism, one of the oldest monotheistic religions, is rooted in the teachings and commandments of the Torah. Regarding the afterlife, Jewish beliefs have evolved significantly, reflecting the rich tapestry of the religion's historical and cultural contexts, as well as deep theological reflections.

Sheol - The Ancient Concept

In the Hebrew Bible, especially in the older texts, the predominant belief was in Sheol, described as a shadowy and silent realm beneath the Earth. It was not a place of reward or punishment but a neutral realm where all souls went after death, regardless of their actions.

Olam HaBa - The World to Come

Over time and under the influence of surrounding cultures and internal theological developments, the concept of "Olam HaBa," or the World to Come, gained importance and prominence. This is often understood in two ways:

1. **A Heavenly Afterlife:** This is a place where souls experience reward or punishment based on their actions in life. The righteous are said to enjoy the Divine presence, while the wicked face the consequences of their transgressions.

2. **Messianic Age:** For some, "Olam HaBa" refers to a future utopian era on Earth where the Messiah reigns, bringing

peace, understanding, and universal recognition of the One God.

The Doctrine of Resurrection

Particularly prevalent among Orthodox Jews is the belief in the bodily resurrection of the dead, associated with the messianic age. This resurrection is reserved for the righteous and is seen as a reaffirmation of God's justice and mercy. The Amidah, a central Jewish prayer, contains a blessing that praises God as the "resurrector of the dead."

Mystical Interpretations - Kabbalah

Jewish mystical tradition, Kabbalah, introduces intricate concepts about the soul's journey, purification, and eventual reunion with the Divine source. Ideas such as "gilgul" (transmigration or reincarnation of souls) are explored within this framework.

Modern Views

Reform Jews and some Conservatives may view the afterlife metaphorically, considering it as living on through one's legacy or the collective memory of the community. The emphasis is often placed on leading a righteous and meaningful life in the present, leaving a lasting positive impact on the world.

Acknowledging the Mystery

Despite the varied interpretations, many Jews embrace the mystery of the afterlife. There is a humble acknowledgment that human understanding is limited and that only God truly knows what awaits beyond this life.

In Summary

While Judaism offers a spectrum of beliefs about the afterlife, the central emphasis remains on ethical living, righteous actions, and maintaining a covenant relationship with God during one's life. This perspective underscores the importance of moral conduct and adherence to mitzvot (commandments) as a means to live a meaningful life in harmony with divine will.

Beliefs in Other Religions

Many indigenous cultures and tribal societies have unique beliefs about the afterlife, often rooted in ancestor worship, nature, or animism. Some see death as a transition where the deceased become ancestors or spirit guides. Others believe in a specific afterlife realm where the dead continue their existence, perhaps living in a mirror version of our world. Let's explore the views of indigenous and tribal perspectives on the afterlife.

Native American Tribes

Native American tribes' beliefs about the afterlife are varied and deeply rooted in their unique histories, legends, and environments. However, many tribes share a reverence for the natural world and see death as a continuation of life's journey.

- **Lakota Sioux:** They believe in the "Happy Hunting Ground," a paradise where souls live similarly to their earthly existence but without suffering.
- **Navajo:** They conceive of the afterlife as a journey to another phase of existence. They often avoid speaking of the dead for fear of evoking their spirits, which might prevent them from completing the journey to the afterlife.
- **Iroquois:** They believe that the souls of the dead must traverse a difficult path to reach the afterlife, requiring the guidance and prayers of the living to help them in their passage.

African Tribal Religions

Africa, with its vast range of cultures and traditions, presents a rich mosaic of afterlife beliefs.

- **Zulu of South Africa:** They see ancestors, or "Amatongo" or "AbeSithole," as intermediaries between the living and the divine. The dead are believed to live in the spirit world, guiding and protecting their living descendants. Rituals and offerings are performed to honor them and seek their blessings.

- **Akan of Ghana:** They conceive of the soul as composed of different parts. While some aspects of the soul return to the Supreme Being, others remain with the body, and still, others become ancestral spirits that play a vital role in guiding the living.
- **Dogon of Mali:** They believe in the reincarnation of souls, which are reborn in subsequent generations within the same lineage. They also believe that the souls of the deceased reside in specific sacred spaces, often represented by particular trees or rocks.

Pacific Islanders' Beliefs

Indigenous peoples of the Pacific Islands also have unique perspectives.

- **Maori of New Zealand:** They view death as a return to their ancestors, a journey to the ancestral homeland of Hawaiki. This journey is reflected in their funeral rites, where the deceased is farewelled with songs and dances that recount the deeds of their ancestors.
- **Hawaii:** It is believed that the spirits of the deceased may remain on earth if they have unfinished business, appearing as ghosts or influencing events. Revered ancestors, "Aumakua," may be animals like sharks or owls and protect their descendants.

These glimpses into indigenous beliefs highlight the intricate ways in which cultures worldwide address the mysteries of life, death, and what lies beyond. Each belief system offers insights into how different societies understand existence, value the contributions of their ancestors, and seek to find meaning in the vastness of the universe.

Conclusions

Religious belief in an afterlife serves both as a guide on how to live a moral life and as a source of comfort against the fear of mortality. Many of the world's religions share common aspects, such as the need to live a righteous life, the hope for a continuation that may be better or worse (depending on how one has lived), and the reunion with deceased loved ones.

In summary, the diverse religious and cultural perspectives on the afterlife not only enrich our understanding of NDEs but also offer a broader and more varied framework for human experiences in the face of death. This invites us to reflect on how spiritual beliefs and practices can influence our lives and how we approach the mystery of existence. Continued research on these experiences could not only lead to greater scientific understanding but also promote interreligious and intercultural dialogue that values the diversity of human experiences.

Chapter 14: What Happens to the Body After Death: From Physics to Metaphysics

The final journey of the human body begins the moment the heart stops beating and the flow of oxygen to the brain ceases. While the specifics may vary depending on medical and environmental factors, the decomposition process generally follows a well-defined sequence.

Decomposition of the Body

The first sign of death is "pallor mortis," characterized by the pale appearance of the skin due to the cessation of blood circulation. This phenomenon occurs within 15-30 minutes after death, as the blood, no longer propelled by the heart, pools in the lower parts of the body due to gravity (known as livor mortis), leaving the upper and visible areas of the body without color. Pallor mortis is often the first visible indicator that death has occurred, but it is not highly precise for estimating the time of death.

Following pallor mortis, rigor mortis sets in, typically beginning 2 to 6 hours after death, depending on environmental conditions and the individual's physical state. Rigor mortis is caused by biochemical changes in the muscles after death, specifically the depletion of adenosine triphosphate (ATP), leading to the permanent binding of actin and myosin, two muscle proteins responsible for muscle contraction. This binding causes the hardening and stiffness of the muscles. Rigor mortis starts in smaller muscles, such as those in the eyelids and jaw, and then spreads throughout the body. The stiffness peaks around 12 hours after death and can persist for up to 72 hours, after which tissues begin to decompose, and the muscles relax again.

Algor mortis refers to the cooling of the body after death. Immediately following death, the body begins to lose heat, as metabolic heat production ceases. The rate at which the body cools is influenced by numerous factors, including ambient temperature, humidity, body mass, and clothing. Generally, the body temperature decreases by about 1-1.5°C per hour until it reaches the ambient temperature, although this rate can vary. Algor mortis is useful for estimating the time of death, but it must be considered alongside other signs for an accurate estimation.

In the days and weeks following death, the body enters the process of putrefaction, the most evident and advanced stage of decomposition. This process is driven by saprophytic bacteria, naturally present in the intestines and other parts of the body, which begin to break down the soft tissues. Putrefaction is characterized by various stages, starting with the chromatic phase, where discoloration of the skin occurs (greenish patches on the abdomen due to hydrogen sulfide production), followed by the gaseous phase, where gas buildup causes the body to bloat. This is followed by the liquefaction phase, in which tissues liquefy, and finally, the skeletal phase, where only bones remain.

The time it takes for the body to reduce to bones can vary significantly depending on various environmental and biological factors, such as humidity, temperature, and the presence of insects and scavengers. In high humidity and warm temperatures, the decomposition process is accelerated, while in cold or arid environments, it can be significantly slowed. Interactions with necrophagous insects, such as flies and beetles, and with predators or scavengers can further influence the decomposition process, contributing to the rapid removal of soft tissues and the skeletonization of the body.

The Fate of the Soul: The Visions of Emanuel Swedenborg

The fate of the soul or spirit after death is a topic that invites deep philosophical, spiritual, and religious reflection. Emanuel Swedenborg, an 18th-century Swedish scientist, philosopher, and theologian, described numerous spiritual experiences and detailed visions of the afterlife. Swedenborg claimed that the soul, remaining conscious after death, finds itself in a transitional realm known as the "World of Spirits," where individuals undergo profound self-examination and are drawn toward heaven or hell based on their true essence and inner desires.

According to Swedenborg, the "World of Spirits" is neither heaven nor hell but a place of reflection and preparation. People shed the masks worn in life, revealing their true selves. Over time, they are drawn to communities of like-minded souls, ascending to heaven or descending to hell, in states that are neither divine rewards nor punishments, but personal choices based on each individual's inner nature.

The Afterlife Visions of Maria Valtorta

The Christian mystic Maria Valtorta, in her writings, describes episodes where Jesus speaks to her about heaven, hell, and purgatory. Her visions of the afterlife are sometimes embedded in dialogues between Jesus and his disciples or as part of her deep mystical contemplations. Here are some significant details:

- **Heaven:** Valtorta describes Heaven primarily through the words of Jesus, depicting it as a place of perfect bliss, where souls enjoy the direct and perpetual vision of God. The souls are free from all suffering, completely immersed in divine love, and live in a state of continuous and undisturbed joy.

- **Hell:** According to Valtorta, hell is described by Jesus as a place of eternal separation from God, where the souls of the damned suffer indescribable torments, not only physical but also spiritual. The essence of hellish punishment is the acute and permanent awareness of having lost God forever.

- **Purgatory:** Valtorta illustrates Purgatory as a place of purification, where souls not fully purified in earthly life undergo necessary sufferings and purgations to prepare for the final encounter with God in Heaven. Here too, pain is present, but it is always accompanied by the hope of salvation and future eternal bliss.

Valtorta emphasizes that these visions were shown to her not only for her personal edification but also to offer a message to others, reminding them of the importance of a virtuous life and the reality of existence beyond death. Her descriptions, rich in detail, are often intertwined with theological and moral lessons.

Despite her unique approach and the richness of details, Valtorta's works remain the subject of debate regarding their authenticity and value as devotional texts rather than doctrinal sources. However, for many readers, her visions continue to be a source of inspiration and a window into a deeply personal and vivid way of understanding Christian teachings.

The journey that follows the death of the physical body, from decomposition to the potential destinations of the soul, reflects a complex intersection between science and spirituality. While science provides us with a detailed understanding of the physical processes that occur after death, the spiritual visions of figures like Emanuel Swedenborg and Maria Valtorta offer fascinating perspectives on what might happen to our immaterial essence.

These explorations, spanning from physics to metaphysics, not only enrich our understanding of death but also invite us to reflect deeply on the meaning of life and consciousness. In this way, our journey through science and spirituality helps us build a more comprehensive and integrated vision of our existence.

Communication with the Deceased

Communication with the deceased is a topic that has always fascinated humanity, evoking hope, curiosity, and skepticism. Through mediums, seances, signs, and dreams, people have sought ways to connect with the afterlife. Modern parapsychology explores phenomena such as Electronic Voice Phenomena (EVP), where unidentified voices are recorded on electronic devices, interpreted by some as messages from the afterlife and by others as mere interference.

Cultural and Spiritual Practices

Various cultures offer rituals and practices for communicating with the deceased, often including prayers, meditations, and ceremonies aimed at creating a bridge between the world of the living and the dead. In many traditions, ancestor worship plays a central role, with rites and offerings intended to honor and appease the spirits of the deceased.

The Catholic Perspective

The Catholic Church has a well-defined position on communication with the deceased, rooted in doctrine and ecclesiastical tradition. Praying for the dead is a fundamental element of Catholic faith, based on the belief in the communion of saints. This communion includes the faithful on earth (the Church Militant), those in purgatory (the Church Penitent), and the saints in heaven (the Church Triumphant).

- **Prayer for the Dead:** Praying for the dead, especially through the sacrifice of the Mass, is seen as a means of assisting the souls in purgatory in their process of purification. The Church teaches that such prayers can help expedite the passage of souls from purgatory to heaven, offering comfort and hope to the living.

- **Direct Communication with the Deceased:** The Catholic Church maintains a cautious and often critical stance regarding direct communication with the deceased through mediums, seances, or other forms of spiritualism. These practices are generally discouraged and often condemned, as they can open the door to spiritual deception and contradict Christian teachings on prayer and the relationship with God. The Catechism of the Catholic Church clearly states that all forms of divination and attempts to evoke the dead are sinful.

- **Apparitions and Saints:** Marian apparitions and those of other saints, which have been officially recognized by the Church after rigorous examination, represent an exception to this general prohibition. In such cases, it is believed that

God allows a saint to appear to the living to offer messages of guidance and hope. However, these apparitions are always subject to careful evaluation by ecclesiastical authority to avoid errors of interpretation and fraud.

The Role of Saints in the Catholic Church

Saints play a crucial role in Catholic tradition as intercessors between God and humanity. Venerated for their holiness and virtue, saints are considered models of Christian life and intermediaries who can present the prayers of the faithful to God. The Catholic Church celebrates numerous feasts dedicated to the saints, and many faithful turn to them in prayer for protection, guidance, and miracles.

- **Prayers and Masses for the Dead:** For Catholics, the most appropriate and safe way to maintain a connection with the deceased is through prayer, especially offering Masses for the repose of souls. Rather than seeking direct communication, the Church teaches to trust in God's mercy and to practice acts of charity and spiritual offerings for the benefit of the souls in purgatory.

Conclusion

Communication with the deceased, while fascinating, must be approached with caution and respect for spiritual and doctrinal guidelines. The Catholic perspective emphasizes prayer as a bridge between the living and the dead, highlighting the importance of entrusting the deceased to divine mercy rather than attempting to establish direct contact through unapproved means. This approach not only respects God's sovereignty over the afterlife but also seeks to protect the faithful from potential spiritual deception.

Chapter 15: Subjective Experiences of Contact with the Deceased and Induced After Death Communication (IADC)

The loss of a loved one is an experience that can deeply scar the human soul, leaving emotional wounds that often do not heal with time. The pain, sadness, and sense of emptiness that follow bereavement can become an oppressive burden, negatively affecting daily life and hindering the healing process. In this context, the technique developed by Allan Botkin, known as Induced After Death Communication (IADC), emerges as an innovative and powerful therapeutic resource, capable of alleviating the pain of grief and offering a new perspective on loss.

The Genesis of IADC: An Innovation Discovered by Chance

Allan Botkin, a clinical psychologist specializing in the treatment of post-traumatic stress disorder (PTSD), developed IADC in 1995 during his therapy sessions with Vietnam War veterans. The technique was born as a variant of Eye Movement Desensitization and Reprocessing (EMDR), a widely recognized and evidence-based therapeutic method for treating trauma. However, IADC differs significantly from the standard EMDR protocol.

The discovery happened almost by accident when, during an EMDR session, a patient reported experiencing contact with a deceased loved one. Initially regarded by Botkin as an unusual phenomenon, this event proved to be recurring and replicable, leading the therapist to refine the technique and develop the IADC protocol.

What Are Subjective Experiences of Contact with the Deceased (VSCD)?

Subjective Experiences of Contact with the Deceased (VSCD) are experiences where individuals perceive they are in contact with a deceased person, often a family member or close friend. These experiences can include a sense of presence, visions, inner dialogues, or the impression of receiving a specific message from the deceased. Despite their subjective nature, VSCDs are described by many as extraordinarily real and deeply consoling experiences, capable of bringing a sense of peace and emotional resolution.

Botkin explains that IADC does not directly induce VSCDs but creates a psychological environment conducive to their emergence. By reducing the intense sadness and pain associated with grief, IADC facilitates a mental state of calm and openness, in which about two-thirds of patients report experiencing a profound connection with the deceased. This connection can manifest through sensory perceptions (sight, hearing, smell, taste) or as a perceived "presence" of the departed loved one.

The Technique of Induced After Death Communication

IADC is a brief psychotherapeutic intervention, generally consisting of two sessions lasting about 90 minutes each, conducted by a qualified therapist. During an IADC session, the therapist guides the patient through a series of eye movements similar to those used in EMDR. This bilateral brain stimulation helps process the painful emotions associated with grief, reducing the intensity of the pain and allowing the patient to reach a state of greater openness and receptivity.

The core of IADC lies in its ability to create conditions for a potential experience of contact with the deceased. Although there is no guarantee that such contact will occur, patients who experience a VSCD during IADC report significant relief from pain and a sense of emotional closure that would otherwise be difficult to achieve.

Effectiveness of IADC in Treating Grief and Trauma

IADC has proven particularly effective in treating complicated grief, a form of grief that is prolonged and prevents the individual from resuming normal life. Many patients report that, thanks to IADC, they were able to overcome the pain and sadness that afflicted them, achieving a new form of acceptance and serenity.

The results of the first experimental study on IADC, conducted by Dr. Janice M. Holden and colleagues and published in *Grief Matters: The Australian Journal of Grief and Bereavement*, showed that patients treated with IADC experienced significantly greater improvement in grief symptoms compared to those who participated in traditional counseling sessions. Statistical analyses indicated that 40% of the variance in grief symptoms was directly attributable to differences in treatments, confirming the effectiveness of IADC.

A Growing Approach: The Spread of IADC Worldwide

Today, IADC is used by a growing number of psychotherapists worldwide to treat grief and emotional trauma. Researchers and therapists in various countries, including Italy and Australia, are conducting studies to further understand and validate this technique. The Italian IADC Research Group, led by Dr. Claudio Lalla, and a study at the University of Adelaide, conducted by Dr. Tom Nehmy, are just a few examples of global efforts to explore and further validate IADC.

In 2020, Allan Botkin announced his retirement, entrusting the leadership of the International IADC Therapy Board to César Valdez, MSW, and Dr. Noelle St. Germain-Sehr, two highly experienced professionals in psychotherapy and grief treatment. Under their guidance, IADC continues to grow and evolve, offering hope and healing to those afflicted by the loss of a loved one.

Psychological and Philosophical Implications of IADC

Induced After Death Communication also raises interesting questions on psychological and philosophical levels. What does it really mean to come into contact with a deceased person? Is it possible that these experiences are a psychological defense mechanism, designed to protect the psyche from the unbearable pain of loss? Or, as some suggest, could IADC reveal something deeper about the nature of consciousness and the existence of a dimension beyond death?

Regardless of the answers to these questions, what is certain is that IADC represents a new frontier in the psychotherapy of grief and trauma. Its ability to alleviate pain and offer comfort to patients is undeniable, and the technique continues to gain popularity among psychotherapists worldwide.

IADC as a New Approach to Grief and Trauma

The discovery of Induced After Death Communication by Allan Botkin has opened up new possibilities in the field of psychotherapy. IADC not only offers an innovative method for treating grief and emotional trauma but also challenges our traditional conceptions of life and death. Through IADC, many patients have found a new way to cope with loss, rediscovering a sense of peace and emotional continuity that would otherwise have been denied to them.

In a world where death is often a taboo, IADC invites us to explore the boundaries between the world of the living and the deceased with courage and an open mind, offering tangible hope to those who are burdened by the pain of loss.

References

Botkin A. Induced After Death Communication: A Miraculous Therapy for Grief and Loss. Humpton Riads Publishing; 2014.

Valdez C, Jordan JR, Botkin A. Induced After-Death Communication. Routledge; 2021.

Conclusions: Personal Reflections and Key Messages

Throughout history, theology, personal testimonies, and scientific investigations, the concept of the afterlife emerges not only as a deeply ingrained element in the human psyche but also as a continuously evolving tapestry of beliefs, hopes, and inquiries. Whether it is the promise of paradise, the cycle of reincarnation, or the mysteries of consciousness explored by neuroscientists, the desire to understand what lies beyond life is a universal theme that fascinates humanity.

Key Messages of the Book

- **Universality of Belief:** Every culture, religion, and civilization has questioned life, death, and what follows. This universal desire reflects the innate curiosity of the human spirit to understand the unknown and find comfort in the face of mortality.

- **Diversity of Visions:** While belief in the afterlife is common across cultures, interpretations vary widely. Each religious and cultural tradition offers its unique perspective on the mysteries of death and the afterlife, shaped by its historical, social, and theological context.

- **Scientific Endeavors:** The dialogue between spirituality and science is becoming increasingly fruitful. Studying near-death experiences, consciousness, and brain activity during death provides valuable insights into the biological and psychological mechanisms that characterize these liminal states.

- **Personal Narratives:** Individual testimonies of near-death experiences or profound spiritual moments related to death offer compelling glimpses that suggest the existence of dimensions beyond the obvious aspects of human life.

- **The Value of Life:** Regardless of what awaits us beyond, beliefs about the afterlife shape our moral, ethical, and spiritual decisions in the present, emphasizing the importance of living a life full of meaning and purpose.

Some Personal Reflections

Writing this book has been much more than just an academic endeavor for me; it has been a journey of personal discovery. The premature loss of my father ignited my curiosity about these themes, driving me to delve deeply into various conceptions of the afterlife. This exploration has broadened my understanding and enriched my worldview.

I have learned to appreciate not only the universal questions we all ask about the afterlife but also the unique nuances that each culture and individual brings to this vast mosaic of beliefs and experiences. While I do not have all the answers—and truly, who does?—I have reached a greater sense of understanding and peace.

The Journey Continues…

The journey does not end here. As science advances and humanity continues to share, reflect, and seek, our understanding of the afterlife evolves. However, one thing remains unchanged: our innate desire to understand our place in the universe and the hope that our existence, in some way, transcends the boundaries of earthly life.

A Message to the Readers

To all readers, I hope you find comfort, curiosity, and inspiration within these pages. May every moment be cherished, every truth sought, and may the journey of life be approached with curiosity and hope. The questions we ask about the meaning of life and what awaits us beyond are, at their core, a reflection of our eternal search for meaning and connection. May you find your answers, and may your journey be illuminated by the same thirst for knowledge that inspired this book.

© Copyright (2024) Dr Francesco Chirico

All Rights Reserved

Printed in Great Britain
by Amazon